The Civil War

Reader

AND HIS

Emancipation Proclamation

Whereas On the Twenty-second day of September, in the year of our Lord one thousand eight hundred and sixty-two, a Proclamation was issued by the President of the United States, containing among other things the following, to-wit:

"That on the first day of January, in the year of our Lord one thousand eight hundred and sixty-three, all persons held as slaves within any State, or designated part of a State, the people whereof shall then be in rebellion against the United States, shall be then, thenceforward and forever free, and the executive government of the United States, including the military and naval authority thereof, will recognize and maintain the freedom of such persons, and will do no act or acts to repress such persons, or any of them, in any efforts they may make for their actual freedom.

"That the executive will, on the first day of January aforesaid, by proclamation, designate the States and parts of States, if any, in which the people thereof respectively shall then be in rebellion against the United States, and the fact that any State, or the people thereof, shall on that day be in good faith represented in the Congress of the United States by members chosen thereto at elections wherein a majority of the qualified voters of such State shall have participated, shall, in the absence of strong countervailing testimony, be deemed conclusive evidence that such State and the people thereof are not then in rebellion against the United States."

Now, therefore, I, ABRAHAM LINCOLN, President of the United States, by virtue of the power in me vested as Commander-in-Chief of the Army and Navy of the United States in time of actual armed rebellion against the authority and government of the United States, and as a fit and necessary war measure for suppressing said rebellion, do, on this first day of January, in the year of our Lord one thousand eight hundred and sixty-three, and in accordance with my purpose so to do, publicly proclaim for the full period of one hundred days from the day the first above mentioned order, and designate as the States and parts of States wherein the people thereof respectively are this day in rebellion against the United States, the following, to-wit:

ARKANSAS, TEXAS, LOUISIANA (except the parishes of St. Bernard, Plaquemines, Jefferson, St. John, St. Charles, St. James, Ascension, Assumption, Terre Bonne, Lafourche, St. Mary, St. Martin, and Orleans, including the city of New Orleans), MISSISSIPPI, ALABAMA, FLORIDA, GEORGIA, SOUTH CAROLINA, NORTH CAROLINA and VIRGINIA (except the forty-eight counties designated as West Virginia, and also the counties of Berkley, Accomac, Northampton, Elizabeth City, York, Princess Ann and Norfolk, including the cities of Norfolk and Portsmouth), and which excepted parts are, for the present, left precisely as if this Proclamation were not issued.

And by virtue of the power and for the purpose aforesaid, I do order and declare that all persons held as slaves within said designated States and parts of States are and henceforward shall be free; and that the executive government of the United States, including the military and naval authorities thereof, will recognize and maintain the freedom of said persons.

And I hereby enjoin upon the people so declared to be free, to abstain from all violence, unless in necessary self-defence, and recommend to them that in all cases, when allowed, they labor faithfully for reasonable wages.

And I further declare and make known that such persons of suitable condition, will be received into the armed service of the United States to garrison forts, positions, stations and other places, and to man vessels of all sorts in said service.

And upon this act, sincerely believed to be an act of justice, warranted by the Constitution, upon military necessity, I invoke the considerate judgment of mankind, and the gracious favor of Almighty God.

In testimony whereof, I have hereunto set my name, and caused the seal of the United States to be affixed.

Done at the City of Washington, this first day of January, in the year of our Lord one thousand eight hundred and sixty-three, and of the Independence of the United States the eighty-Seventh.

By the President: ABRAHAM LINCOLN.

L.S.

WILLIAM H. SEWARD, Secretary of State.

NOTE.—The rest of the slaves were afterwards freed by Legislation and Constitutional Amendments.

Core Knowledge®

ISBN: 978-1-68380-232-7

The Civil War

Table of Contents

The Civil War
Reader
Core Knowledge History and Geography™

Chapter 1
Slavery

A Remarkable Anniversary The date was July 3, 1826. As the fiftieth anniversary of the Declaration of Independence approached, a great drama was playing itself out in the homes of two of the men most responsible for that document. At Monticello in Virginia, Thomas Jefferson, now age eighty-three, slipped in and out of consciousness as he lay on his deathbed.

The Big Question

Why did the demand for slaves increase in the Southern states?

And in Quincy, Massachusetts, John Adams, now age ninety, also neared the end of his life. Would these two great patriots and former presidents live to see this fiftieth Independence Day? Americans everywhere hoped and prayed that they would.

As midnight arrived, Thomas Jefferson stirred in his bed and whispered to a young relative, "This is the Fourth?" The young man nodded. Jefferson sighed contentedly. He said no more, and by noon he was gone.

Thomas Jefferson

John Adams

At that very moment in Quincy, Massachusetts, the roar of a cannon signaled the start of the town's celebration. John Adams struggled to utter what proved to be his last sentence. His granddaughter, bending close to the old man, was able to hear his final whispered words, "Thomas—Jefferson—still—surv—." Before the sun had set, he too was gone.

In their lifetimes, Thomas Jefferson and John Adams had seen their beloved United States grow from a struggling group of new states into a strong, confident nation. During the fifty years following the Declaration of Independence, the United States had gained vast new lands and developed into a democracy that was a model for countries around the world.

In one important way, however, America had not changed and was not a model at all. Almost from the beginning, even during colonial times, **slavery** had been part of American life. When the thirteen colonies became the first thirteen states,

> **Vocabulary**
>
> **slavery, n.** a system in which people are legally owned by another and forced to work without pay

nearly one in every five Americans was an African American. Nearly all African Americans were enslaved. By far, most of these slaves lived in the South. But there were slaves in the Northern states, too. At the time of the American Revolution, for example, one in every ten New Yorkers was a slave. Slaves in the North worked mainly as house servants for rich families. Now, fifty years later, Southerners wanted to see slavery spread to the new western territories as well.

For a short time after the Declaration of Independence was written, there seemed a slim chance that slavery might die out. That was partly because of the words that lie at the very heart of the Declaration:

*We hold these truths to be **self-evident**; that all men are created equal, that they are endowed by their Creator with certain **unalienable** rights, that among these are life, liberty, and the pursuit of happiness.*

So how could people accept slavery and still live up to the words of the Declaration of Independence? A growing number of Americans, both Northerners and Southerners, believed that they could not. As John Adams wrote to his wife, Abigail, slaves "have as good a right to freedom as we have." Some Americans freed their slaves during the Revolutionary War era. Before long, all the Northern states took steps to end slavery. The Northwest Ordinance banned slavery in five new western states. Congress ended the slave trade in 1808. The Constitution had provided for the end of the slave trade in 1808. No Southern state went so far as to free all the slaves, but a few made it easier for slave owners to free their slaves if they wished to.

The former president, George Washington, owned many slaves at Mount Vernon, his home in Virginia. He and other slave owners who believed that slavery was wrong, declared that when they died, their slaves were to be set free. By the early 1800s, there were about 150,000 free African Americans. Most of them lived in the

Like many others living in the South, George Washington owned slaves on his estate at Mount Vernon.

Southern states. However, for most slaves in the South, freedom was still out of reach.

But not everyone who believed slavery was wrong favored equal **civil rights** for freed African Americans. This was certainly true in the five new western states to which the Northwest Ordinance applied. Ending slavery was one thing. Allowing African Americans to have the full rights of citizens—like voting, holding office, serving on juries, living where they wanted to live, working in whatever jobs they chose—was something else altogether.

While some people, such as Abraham Lincoln, did believe that the rights outlined in the Declaration of Independence extended to people of color—free or enslaved – many did not. For many people, the notion of liberty had more to do with self-government and the possibility of rising up economically than with the removal of racial slavery or with equal rights for people of color.

The Cotton Gin

Despite progress, by 1810, almost no slave owners were willing to free their slaves. What caused the change in attitude? Slaves had become much more valuable. A new invention called the cotton gin now made it even more profitable to use slave labor to grow cotton. Southerners began growing cotton back in the mid-1700s. Cotton, however, was not an important crop at first. That's because the kind of cotton that grows best in the American South is filled with sticky green seeds. Those seeds had to be removed before the cotton could be used. At that time, it took a single person a whole day to clean the seeds from just one pound of cotton. This increased the cost of Southern cotton a great deal. So most makers of cotton goods looked to other parts of the world for their supply of raw cotton.

In 1793, Eli Whitney, a young New Englander who liked to tinker with machines and solve problems, changed all that. That year, Whitney visited a Georgia plantation. The owner of the plantation showed Whitney some freshly picked cotton, complete with green seeds. She suggested that he might like to try to invent something that would remove the seeds more easily.

Whitney did just that, and in only ten days! The invention was a system of combs and brushes on rollers, small enough to fit into a small box. The contraption was powered by turning a handle.

The cotton gin made cotton a profitable crop in the Southern states and territories.

Later, Eli built a larger machine that cleaned up to fifty pounds of cotton a day. Whitney called his machine a cotton engine, or cotton gin for short.

Eli Whitney's invention made it possible for Southerners to sell their cotton cheaply. Factories in the North, and especially in Great Britain, were now ready to buy all the cotton the South could grow. Soon, planters started large plantations on rich lands in the Mississippi and Alabama territories. Cotton quickly became the South's most important crop. By 1820, the South grew one hundred times as much cotton as it had raised before Eli Whitney built his cotton gin.

To grow this cotton, the plantation owners needed more laborers to plow, plant, **cultivate**, and harvest. As a result, slaves were in greater demand than ever. The price of buying a slave doubled. Far from freeing their slaves, Southern planters now sought to buy more slaves.

Vocabulary

cultivate, v. to help grow

Chapter 2
The Life of the Slave

Slavery in the South What was life like for slaves in the American South? Much depended on where they worked and who owned them. Slaves on small farms usually worked in the fields alongside their owners. They did many other tasks, too. On a small farm, everyone did a little bit of everything.

The Big Question
....
How did slaves in the South resist?

On large plantations, however, slaves usually did only one task. A small number worked and lived in the great house with the master's family. These house servants cooked, cleaned, and did other housework. They also helped raise the master's children. Some other slaves became skilled carpenters, blacksmiths, brick makers, and barrel makers. By far, however, most slaves on a large plantation worked in the fields.

Enslaved men, women, and children worked in the fields on large plantations.

Whether they lived on a small farm or a great plantation, slaves worked from dawn until dusk. Hard work, however, is not what made slavery a terrible thing. After all, many people who were not slaves also worked hard.

No, what made slavery wrong was that slaves were not free. They did not have, as in the words of the Declaration of Independence, the right to "life, liberty,

and the pursuit of happiness." Another person owned them without their **consent** and was their master. Another person owned their labor and the fruits of that labor.

An owner could treat his slaves like pieces of property. He could buy them; he could sell them. He could sell some members of a slave family and not others, or sell husbands and wives and children to different buyers. In fact, three in every ten slave families were broken up by such sales.

Slaves could be whipped for not working hard enough or fast enough, or for not showing proper respect to members of their owner's family, or for many other small reasons—sometimes for no reason at all. Not all owners were this cruel, but some certainly were. Violence was essential to the slave system, or the slaves would stop working for free and walk away.

In addition, slaves could not leave the plantation without their owner's permission. Only the kindest and most unusual of owners allowed their slaves to be educated. In many states, it was illegal to teach slaves to read and write. A famous slave

Slave children were not allowed to be educated.

named Frederick Douglass later said he recovered his manhood and humanity when he learned to read.

Slave Resistance

Slave owners told themselves, and anyone else who would listen, that their slaves were happy. And probably some of these slave owners actually believed that. Of course, if the slaves were really happy being slaves, they would not have fought against the slavery system. But they did. A few slaves organized uprisings, or rebellions. One such person was Nat Turner. Turner was the slave of a plantation owner in Virginia. His master's family thought of him as a religious, peaceful man—until one day in 1831. On that day, Nat Turner led a group of slaves in an uprising. Over the next three days, he and his followers killed fifty-five men, women, and children. In the end, all the slaves who took part in Turner's Rebellion were caught, tried, and hanged.

Not many slaves rebelled as Nat Turner did, for they knew they had almost no chance to succeed. Many more slaves simply ran away at one time or another, even though they knew their chances of successfully escaping were not much better. Runaway slaves from Mississippi or Louisiana, for example, would have to cross hundreds of miles in slave states before finally reaching a Northern state where there was no slavery. Chances were that slave catchers, eager to collect rewards, would hunt them down long before they could reach freedom. The catchers would return the runaways to their plantations, where they would receive harsh punishment.

Most slaves **resisted** slavery in other ways. Sometimes they would simply work slowly. They would pretend to be ill. They would "accidentally" break tools or set fire to the buildings. Owners suspected that these things had been done on purpose, but they rarely knew for sure.

Of course, slaves did not dare to speak openly of their misery and their longing

> **Vocabulary**
>
> **resist,** v. to fight against; oppose
>
> **resistance,** n. the act of taking a stand against something by way of words or actions

Runaway slaves were hunted down by slave catchers.

for freedom. Instead, they spoke through their songs, called spirituals. If the slave owners really thought their slaves were happy, they could not have been listening very carefully to these songs.

Most spirituals told of the weariness of the slaves and of their hope for a better world to come. Their message was clear in the first few lines. Here are a few: *O brothers, don't get weary; Nobody knows the trouble I've seen;* and *Sometimes I feel like a motherless child.* Those are not the words of happy people grateful to have masters to take care of them.

In some spirituals, slaves expressed their longing to be free. Doing that openly was dangerous, so they used code words, such as **deliverance**, to stand for freedom from slavery. This is one such spiritual:

> **Vocabulary**
>
> **deliverance,** n. the action of rescuing someone or setting them free

Didn't my Lord deliver Daniel,

> *deliver Daniel, deliver Daniel?*

Didn't my Lord deliver Daniel?

Then why not every man?

He delivered Daniel from the lion's den,

Jonah from the belly of the whale,

And the Hebrew children from the fiery furnace,

Then why not deliver every man?

Working in the fields from sunup to sundown was not the only thing slaves did, however. After work they returned to their cabins in the slave quarter, or the section of the plantation where they lived. Here, slave families could be by themselves. Even though they were tired, they often raised small gardens or hunted and fished for more variety in their diet other than just pork and corn.

In the slave quarter, slaves created their own community. They told and retold stories and folktales handed down from earlier generations. In many of these stories, a weak character **outwits** a strong one. For example, a clever rabbit might trick a hungry fox. Can you see why such stories would be popular among the slaves? The slaves also kept African music and dancing alive. Some continued to hold on to the religious beliefs and practices of their ancestors in Africa.

> **Vocabulary**
> ....
> **outwit,** v. to outsmart; to win by using trickery

Even slaves who became Christians, as most did, often mixed some African religious beliefs and customs in with their new beliefs. And as they blended elements of African cultures with American culture, they created something new and different— the beginnings of a unique African American culture.

The trickster rabbit was a popular character in folk tales shared in the slave community.

Chapter 3
The Missouri Compromise

The Spread of Slavery By the early 1800s, Southern slaveholders demanded that slavery be allowed to spread into America's western lands. Most Northerners were against this idea largely because they wanted to reserve **territories** for white settlers. They opposed the Southern slave owners' demands. In the end, this disagreement between the North and the South would become one of the major issues that led to the Civil War.

The Big Question

How did the Missouri Compromise attempt to resolve the issue of slavery in the territories?

Vocabulary

territory, n. an area of land

compromise, n. when each side in a dispute gives up some of their demands to reach an agreement

Before then, however, the two sections of the country tried to settle their disagreement through **compromise**. To understand this issue, it's important to know about the differences between states and territories in the history of the United States. Today, the United States of America has fifty states. Each has its own state constitution, and each makes many of its own laws.

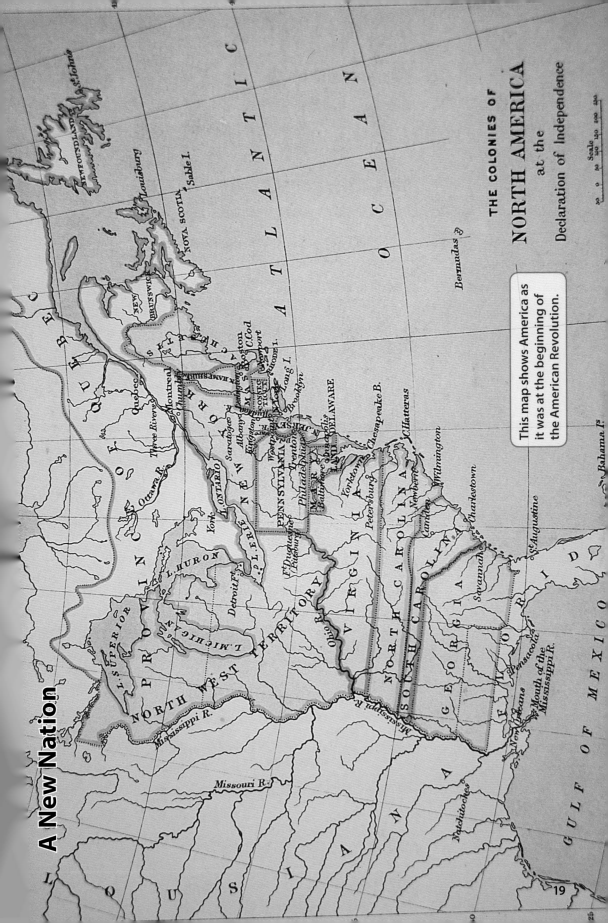

A New Nation

THE COLONIES OF
NORTH AMERICA
at the
Declaration of Independence

Scale
20 0 20 40 100 200 300

This map shows America as
it was at the beginning of
the American Revolution.

19

In the beginning, though, there were only thirteen states. The other states were formed over a period of time from the huge chunks of land that the United States gained from countries such as Great Britain, France, and Mexico.

Early in the history of the United States, Congress wisely decided to set up a three-step process for turning those lands into states. In the first step, Congress created a territory, or sometimes several territories. As a part of this first step, Congress made the laws for the territory. The second step came when the population of a territory reached five thousand adult males. Then the people were allowed to elect their own representatives and make many of their own laws. When a territory's population reached sixty thousand free inhabitants, it could ask Congress to be admitted into the **Union** with its own state constitution. That was the third and final step—the step that allowed a territory to become a state.

> **Vocabulary**
>
> **Union,** n. the states that made up the United States of America; during the Civil War the states that supported the U.S. government
>
> **statehood,** n. the condition of being a state in the United States

In those days, each state decided for itself whether to allow slavery within its borders. Southern states allowed slavery. Most Northern states did not. But for territories, slavery was a different matter. During a territory's first step toward **statehood**, it was Congress that made all the rules, including whether to allow slavery.

Suppose Congress voted *not* to allow slavery in a territory. Would anyone who owned slaves or who wanted to own slaves choose to live there? Certainly not. So when the population became large enough for the territory to start making its own laws, almost no one living there would be in favor of slavery, and the new **legislature** would pass laws against it. Later still, when the territory was ready

to become a state, it would write a state constitution that would prevent slavery. Of course, the opposite would happen if Congress permitted slavery when the territory was formed.

Slave or Free?

Regardless of how a person felt about the spread of slavery into the western lands, that first law Congress passed for any territory was important. That is what led to a big argument in 1820 between the North and the South. The argument concerned slavery in the Louisiana Purchase, a huge area that the United States had bought from France. When Congress began to form new territories in this region, it did not make any laws about slavery. Southern slaveholders felt free to move there with their slaves. The first of these new territories to become a state was Louisiana, which entered the Union in 1812 as a slave state. Seven years later a second territory was ready for statehood. This was the Missouri Territory, which also asked to come into the Union as a slave state.

At that time, there were eleven slave states and eleven free states in the Union. The Northern free states were against adding more slave states. They said this would give the South too much power in Congress. "Nonsense," replied the South. Without any more slave states, it was the North that would have too much power in Congress.

Each side was determined not to give in. One New York newspaper editor wrote that the Missouri question "involves not only the future **character** of our nation, but the future weight and influence of the free states. If now lost—it is lost forever."

Vocabulary

character, n. the qualities that make up the personality and behavior of a person or a country

The Missouri Compromise

For more than a year, Congress angrily debated the Missouri question. Finally, in 1820, a compromise was reached. At this time, Maine in northern New England was also ready for statehood. Congress admitted Maine, and just over a year later Missouri was admitted. Maine was admitted as a free state and Missouri as a slave state. That kept the balance between slave and free states. At the same time, Congress drew a line starting at Missouri's southern border, which was at 36°30′ north latitude, straight across the rest of the Louisiana Purchase. Congress prohibited slavery in territories above that line and permitted slavery in territories below it. This came to be known as the Missouri Compromise.

For the time being, the Missouri Compromise quieted the anger over the spread of slavery. By making a law that dealt with slavery in all the remaining western lands owned by the United States, Congress thought it had settled the slavery question once and for all.

Time would show how wrong Congress was.

Slave and Non Slave States

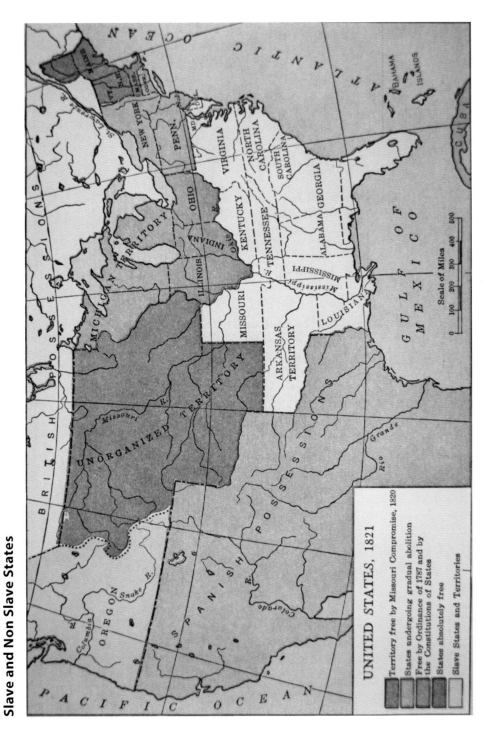

UNITED STATES, 1821

Scale of Miles
0 100 200 300 400 500

Territory free by Missouri Compromise, 1820
States undergoing gradual abolition
Free by Ordinance of 1787 and by the Constitutions of States
States absolutely free
Slave States and Territories

The Missouri Compromise attempted to settle the question of the spread of slavery.

Chapter 4
Growth of Antislavery Feeling

A Terrible Wrong Today, most people would agree that slavery is a terrible wrong. It is wrong that one person can actually own another. It is wrong that a person can buy and sell someone like a piece of property.

The Big Question

How did abolitionists and the people of the Underground Railroad fight against slavery?

In ancient Greece, slaves were used in much the same way as slaves in the United States. They worked in the fields and in people's homes. They were often treated harshly.

25

It's hard to understand that not everyone has always felt this way. But the sad fact is that slavery has existed in many times and places, including in ancient Greece and ancient Rome, in Africa, in parts of Europe during the Middle Ages, and elsewhere. It's been only in the last 250 years, really, that a growing number of people have come to believe that slavery is unacceptable. And even when many people finally began to believe that slavery was wrong, few were ready to do anything to get rid of it.

The first chapter explained how a number of slaveholders, moved by the words of the Declaration of Independence, freed their slaves. In the early 1800s, however, few slave owners were willing to do so. And while many people in the North didn't want to see slavery spread any farther, very few raised their voices against it where it already existed. That is why Congress believed that, in passing the Missouri Compromise, they had ended the argument about slavery once and for all.

But by the 1820s a small number of Americans began to speak out against slavery in general. Some searched for practical ways to end the practice. Some simply tried to persuade owners to treat their slaves more like human beings than like property. Others hoped to get more owners to agree that after they died, their slaves would become free. Still others believed that slavery might be ended gradually by paying owners who agreed to give up their slaves. Ending slavery in this way would take many, many years. Most politicians agreed that the states controlled whether there was slavery in the South. They believed that Congress and the president had no authority to end it there. Southern states would have to act voluntarily, or there would have to be a **constitutional amendment**, to end slavery.

Abolitionists

There was another small group, however, that wanted to abolish, or put an end to slavery entirely and immediately. These people came to be called **abolitionists**. One of their leaders was William Lloyd Garrison.

In 1831, Garrison started a newspaper called *The Liberator* to carry his message to other Americans. Garrison was a deeply

> **Vocabulary**
>
> **"constitutional amendment,"** (phrase) an official change or addition to the Constitution
>
> **abolitionist,** n. a person who worked to end slavery during the 1700s and 1800s

religious man. In the very first issue of *The Liberator*, Garrison let readers know what kind of message to expect from him. "I will be as harsh as truth," he wrote, "and as uncompromising as justice." Garrison meant that he would write about the cruelty of slavery, without prettying it up. "I will not excuse," he wrote. "I will not retreat a single inch—*and I will be heard*." He took a position that allowed no room for compromise on the issue.

True to his word, in issue after issue of *The Liberator*, Garrison described the cruelty of slavery and urged his readers to take steps to end slavery right away. Garrison also helped organize the American Anti-Slavery Society in 1833.

Another important abolitionist leader was Frederick Douglass. Douglass was once a slave himself, but he learned to read and

In his newspaper *The Liberator*, (top of page), William Lloyd Garrison argued for the abolition, or end, of slavery. Frederick Douglass, (above), spoke of the horrors of slavery.

wanted freedom. He escaped to the North through the **Underground Railroad**. He became friends with Garrison and soon began giving talks about his life as a slave. In one speech he recalled the slave trade in Baltimore, where he lived before escaping

to freedom. "In the deep, still darkness of midnight," said Douglass, "I have been often aroused by the dead, heavy footsteps, and the piteous cries of the chained gangs that passed our door . . . on the way to the slave markets, where the victims are to be sold like horses, sheep, and swine. . . . My soul sickens at the sight."

What powerful words! How Douglass's listeners must have been moved by them! Douglass also wrote a book in which he told the story of his life and his escape from slavery. Later he started an antislavery newspaper of his own in the city of Rochester, New York.

At first, abolitionists were a very small group. In fact they never actually grew to be more than a tiny minority of the white population. Across the country, only a few thousand people bought Garrison's newspaper. Most of them were free African Americans who hardly needed to be told that slavery was bad. Not many people bought Frederick Douglass's book, either.

Not surprisingly, Garrison's attacks on slavery and the Southern way of life angered Southerners. But Garrison's attacks angered many people in the North, too. Many Northerners were not yet ready to hear Garrison's abolitionist message. To them, Garrison, Douglass, and the other abolitionists were a bunch of troublemakers. Several times, angry mobs broke up public meetings at which abolitionists were speaking. They attacked abolitionist speakers and sometimes beat them. Once a mob dragged Garrison through the streets of Boston, where he was visiting to give an abolitionist speech.

In time, however, the number of people who agreed with the abolitionists grew. More Northerners came to agree that slavery was evil and that somehow, in some way, it must be ended.

The Underground Railroad

Some people were already striking a blow against slavery. These were the members of the Underground Railroad. The Underground Railroad was not an actual railroad with trains. It was a network of people who helped runaway slaves escape to free states in the North or to Canada. These people offered their homes, cellars, barns, and places of work to hide runaways. At each such "station" on the railroad, the runaway slaves, or "passengers," rested and received instructions for getting to the next station. The people who hid the slaves and guided them on their journey were known as "conductors."

One of the most famous conductors was a runaway slave who had taken the Underground Railroad to freedom herself. Her name was Harriet Tubman. In 1849, Harriet Tubman was living on a Maryland plantation when she learned that her owner had died. The death of a slave owner was very dangerous for slaves because that was when they were most likely to be sold. Would families be sold together, or would they be split up? Would the new owners be kind, or would they be cruel? These questions were impossible to answer.

Harriet Tubman decided not to wait to find out. Late one night she went to the home of a white woman who had promised to help her escape. The woman sent Harriet to another white family a few miles away. There, the woman who welcomed her quickly gave Harriet a broom and told her to sweep the yard so that anyone seeing her in the daytime would think she was a slave. Later that night, the woman's husband drove Harriet in his wagon to the next town, where yet another family took her in.

In this way, hiding by day and traveling by night, Harriet made her way north until she crossed the border between Maryland and Pennsylvania. This border was also known as the Mason-Dixon line. During colonial times, two **surveyors** named Charles Mason and Jeremiah Dixon drew this line. In time the Mason-Dixon line, separating

> **Vocabulary**
>
> surveyor, n. a worker who measures and examines land

the slave state of Maryland from the free state of Pennsylvania, came to have a new meaning. And now that Harriet Tubman had crossed it, she was in Pennsylvania, where slavery was prohibited. Harriet Tubman was a free woman at last!

The next year, Harriet Tubman joined the Underground Railroad. Over the next ten years, she made nineteen trips into the South to "conduct" slaves to freedom. During those years, she led about three hundred slaves to the North. She knew all kinds of tricks to help her passengers escape. She usually started her rescues on a Saturday night, knowing that it would be Monday before the owners could spread the alarm with posters and advertisements. Traveling by night, she looked to the North Star to find the right direction. On cloudy nights, when stars could not be seen, she would feel the bark of trees to find the soft moss because moss grows on the north side.

The slaves called Harriet Tubman "Moses" because she delivered them from slavery. In the South, a reward of $12,000 was offered for her capture. No one was ever able to collect it. Many years later, when she looked back on her work in the Underground Railroad, Harriet Tubman said, "I never ran my train off the track, and I never lost a passenger."

Although Harriet Tubman looked back with pride on her success in leading runaway slaves to freedom, only a small number of slaves achieved freedom through the Underground Railroad.

Conductors, such as Harriet Tubman, led runaway slaves north using guides, such as the North Star.

Chapter 5
Growing Apart

Differences Between North and South The North and the South continued to disagree over the issue of slavery. Despite this disagreement, it's important to understand that Americans were still one people. They shared a common language, and for many, a common faith. They honored their shared history, especially their Revolutionary achievement. But other social changes were beginning to lead many people to believe that the North and the South were growing further apart.

The Big Question

What were the economic differences between the North and the South?

The British invention of machines that spun cotton faster than people changed the cotton industry in America.

More people in the North now lived in towns and cities. Most Southerners still farmed for a living. In the North, **manufacturing** was growing increasingly important. And at this time in Great Britain, major changes were taking place in clothmaking. There several men invented machines that spun cotton into thread *two hundred times faster* than a person using a spinning wheel. Soon after, others invented a machine that could weave the thread into hundreds of yards of cloth in a single day.

Before long, British manufacturers constructed buildings called factories, or **mills**, to house these new machines. Power to run the machines came from swiftly flowing streams that turned the waterwheels attached to the new machines.

With these machines, British manufacturers produced cloth faster, cheaper, and better than anyone else. The British government was determined to keep this advantage. The government would not let anyone sell the new machines to other countries or make plans to take them out of the country. The government even passed a law that said people who worked in cotton mills were not allowed to leave Great Britain.

Keeping such a large secret, though, is nearly impossible. Sooner or later the secret gets out. In this case it was sooner. Several American manufacturers placed an advertisement in a British newspaper offering a reward to anyone who could build a spinning machine for them. Samuel Slater, a young employee in a British spinning mill, saw the ad. After memorizing every part of the machine, the twenty-one-year-old Slater disguised himself as a farm boy and boarded a ship headed for the United States in 1789.

It took Slater two years to make every wooden part of the machine by hand. In 1791, he finished the job. The machine worked. That year, America's first cotton thread mill opened in Pawtucket, Rhode Island. Some years after, a wealthy Boston

Samuel Slater's mill was the first cotton mill in America.

merchant named Francis Lowell and several wealthy friends built a large factory in which machines not only spun the cotton thread but also dyed it and wove it into cloth.

Soon dozens, then hundreds, of other factories sprang up. Most of these early factories were located in New England. The rushing water of New England's many rivers and streams were used to power the machines. Later, factories spread to other parts of the Northeast. The factories made more than just cloth. They also made shoes, pots and pans, household goods, and farm machinery. The goods traveled from the factories by canals and railroads to hundreds of thousands of family farms in the North and West. Farmers paid for the goods by shipping their wheat, corn, barley, and other crops to markets in the East on those same canals and railroads. From there, many of those crops were sent by ship to other countries.

All this new manufacturing and trade led to the rapid growth of cities in the North. At the time of the American Revolution, there were only five cities in the whole country. The largest city, Philadelphia, had fewer than forty thousand residents. New York was the second largest, with fewer than twenty thousand. By 1850, however, nearly one hundred places in the United States could call themselves cities. Nearly all of them were in the North and in the region we call the Midwest. New York alone had a half million people. Philadelphia, in Pennsylvania, was not far behind. Pittsburgh, also in Pennsylvania, Chicago in Illinois, and Cincinnati in Ohio were also growing rapidly. In these cities, people could find jobs.

The Rural South

The South, meanwhile, grew in a different direction. There were some factories in the South, but not many. The same was true for railroads. The number of large Southern cities could be counted on one hand. The great majority of Southerners made their living from the land. While the North was gradually becoming more **urban**, the South remained **rural**.

Southerners believed their future lay with cotton. They were sure that the increasing demand for cotton from factories in the North and in Great Britain would make the South wealthy and strong. A Northerner with money might start a new business or build a factory, but a Southerner would buy more land to grow cotton. He would also buy more slaves to work that land.

A few of these big cotton farmers, or planters, owned very large farms. These large farms, or plantations, were much larger than the family farms of the North and the West. These plantation owners were the leaders of the South. They lived in large mansions, had many household servants, and entertained friends and relatives in the manner of wealthy people. Each planter owned fifty or more slaves.

Of course, the great planters' grand lifestyle was built on the labor of African American slaves. So, it is not surprising that at the very time more Northerners opposed slavery, the leading families of the South were more determined to keep it.

Some Southern plantations were very large. Slaves worked in the fields, in workshops on the plantation, and in the plantation owner's house.

Not all farmers lived on large plantations though. The majority of Southern farmers owned small farms, and some struggled to grow enough food. Though they generally supported slavery and some owned one or two slaves, they did not live rich, comfortable lives.

By the 1840s, most Northerners opposed the spread of slavery into the territories. Most Southerners demanded that slavery be allowed to spread. The stage was set for trouble should the United States ever gain more territory in the West. But that's just what happened as a result of the war with Mexico. The argument that followed over the spread of slavery into that new territory almost broke up the Union.

Chapter 6
A House Divided

The Big Question In 1846, the United States and Mexico went to war over disputed land in the Southwest. In less than a year, the United States gained California and New Mexico. When the war ended in 1848, the United States had gained much of the Southwest. But once again the issue of slavery would present itself. Should this newly acquired land have slavery, or not? The question was of great importance.

The Big Question

Why did compromises fail to solve the national argument about slavery?

Senators held heated debates about the issue of slavery in the new lands gained by America.

The U.S. **senators** debated the question. Should slavery be allowed in the new lands won from Mexico? As you read earlier, whatever Congress decided about a territory pretty much decided what kind of state it would later become—either slave or free. In 1850, there were fifteen of each in the Union. But California asked for **admission** to the Union as a free state. Southerners feared that free states would soon greatly outnumber slave states, especially if Congress did not allow slavery in the new territories. If that happened, they asked, might the Northerners manage to change the Constitution making all slavery illegal, even in the Southern states where it already existed?

Tempers ran high as the arguments went back and forth. "Slaves are property," said Southerners. If Northerners could bring their property into the new territories, why couldn't Southern slaveholders bring theirs? "Because," said Northerners and most Westerners, "slaves are people, not property, and slavery is wrong." The soil of the new western territories was free of slavery when Mexico owned it. Northerners and Westerners argued it should continue to remain free soil. Those who believed that all the western territory should be reserved for free people came to be called "free soilers."

Some senators searched for a compromise. But John C. Calhoun, the South's greatest spokesman, had no interest in compromise. On March 4, 1850, Calhoun, weak and near death, was carried to the Senate floor on a stretcher. There, he handed his speech to a younger senator to read aloud. The North, said Calhoun, must give the South equal rights in the new territories. It must stop criticizing and stirring up trouble over slavery. It must return runaway slaves.

John C. Calhoun

If Northern senators could not agree to these conditions, said Calhoun, then "say so; and let the States we both represent agree to separate and part in peace." Calhoun was saying that the Southern states would **secede**, or pull out of the Union. His next words rang through the halls of the Senate like a clap of thunder: "If you are unwilling we should part in peace, tell us so, and we shall know what to do."

We shall know what to do. No one listening to Calhoun's words failed to understand their meaning: the South was willing to go to war.

Vocabulary

secede, v. to formally withdraw membership

In the end, a compromise was reached. In 1850, California was admitted to the Union as a free state. That satisfied the North. The rest of the land gained from Mexico was divided into two territories, forming New Mexico and Utah. The federal government did not place any restrictions on slavery in the new territories. Instead, the people of each territory would decide the issue for themselves. That satisfied the South.

Another part of the Compromise of 1850 made it illegal to buy and sell slaves in Washington, D.C., the nation's capital. That was something the North wanted. In exchange, the South got a **Fugitive** Slave Law, which made it easier for slave owners to get back fugitive slaves who had escaped to the North.

For the time being, the Compromise of 1850 cooled the argument between North and South. But could that last? Some Southerners were already saying that the South had given up too much and should secede from the Union immediately. Some Northerners, meanwhile, said they would never obey the Fugitive Slave Law and send a fellow human being back into slavery.

Harriet Beecher Stowe

One such Northerner was Harriet Beecher Stowe. Stowe came from a family of New England abolitionists. She wrote a story that showed the cruelty of slavery. Her book, *Uncle Tom's Cabin*, was an immediate sensation. One part of *Uncle Tom's Cabin* tells of a young slave mother, Eliza, who discovers that her baby has been sold and will be taken from her the next day. Eliza makes a desperate dash for freedom with the child and escapes into the free state of Ohio, just ahead of her pursuers.

Published in 1852, more than three hundred thousand copies of *Uncle Tom's Cabin* were sold in the book's first year. Compared to

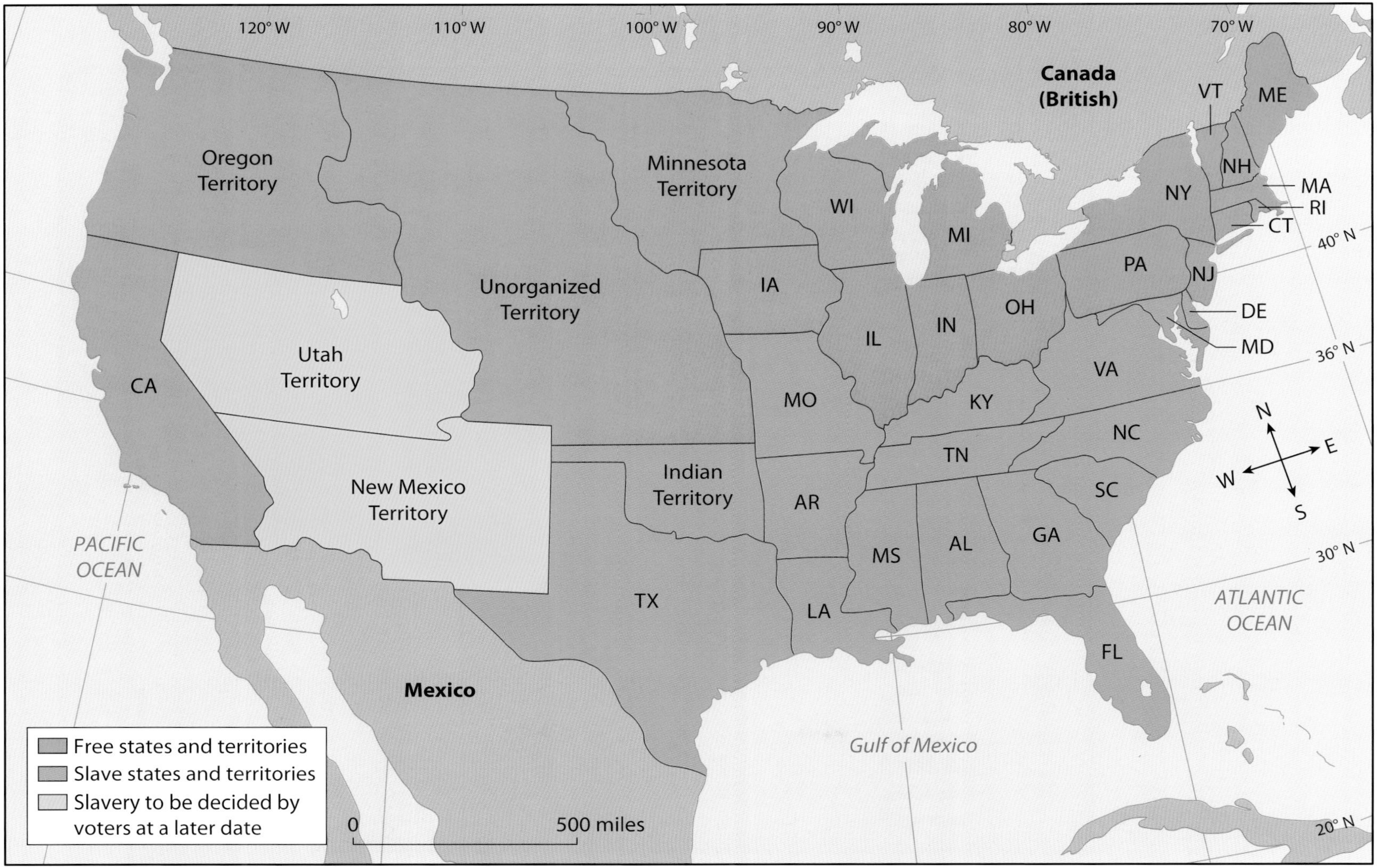

The Compromise of 1850 temporarily calmed tensions over the issue of slavery.

Map labels:

Canada (British)

Mexico

ATLANTIC OCEAN

PACIFIC OCEAN

Gulf of Mexico

Oregon Territory

Minnesota Territory

Unorganized Territory

Utah Territory

New Mexico Territory

Indian Territory

TX

CA

IA

MO

AR

LA

WI

IL

MI

IN

OH

KY

TN

MS

AL

GA

SC

NC

VA

FL

PA

NY

VT

NH

ME

MA

RI

CT

NJ

DE

MD

Legend:
- Free states and territories
- Slave states and territories
- Slavery to be decided by voters at a later date

0   500 miles

20° N, 30° N, 36° N, 40° N

70° W, 80° W, 90° W, 100° W, 110° W, 120° W

N E S W

the present population of the United States, that would be like selling *three million* copies today. The book was translated into twenty languages and was read by millions more people around the world. It was also turned into a play that was performed before large audiences all over the North.

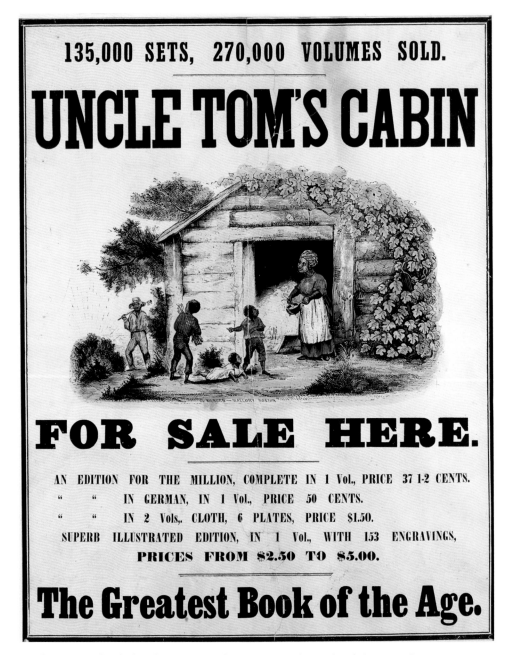

Uncle Tom's Cabin helped many people recognize the evils of slavery. This is a poster advertising the book.

The story and the characters of *Uncle Tom's Cabin* became familiar to millions of Americans. Many Northerners especially were touched by Stowe's book. Southerners said that the book was terribly unfair and gave a false picture of slavery, especially because Stowe had never visited the South. If people like Harriet Beecher Stowe continued to stir up criticism of slavery and the South, the Union was surely doomed.

The Kansas-Nebraska Act

Stephen A. Douglas was one of the ablest men in the U.S. Senate. Many thought of Douglas, a senator from Illinois, as a future president of the United States. But in 1854, Douglas made a decision that may very well have ended his chance to become president. It also led the country toward the Civil War.

That had not been Douglas's intention, of course. He had only wanted to encourage people to move to the one remaining part of the Louisiana Purchase that was still unsettled. This was the huge area between the western boundaries of Missouri and Iowa and the Rocky Mountains, and from the 36° 30' latitude northward to the Canadian border.

If you recall, the Missouri Compromise said that slavery would not be allowed in any territory in the Louisiana Purchase country north of 36° 30' latitude. Also, if a territory chose to remain free, it would almost surely become a free state later. Of course, this was the last thing Southern senators wanted. How, then, could Douglas win their support for his goal of settling this land?

The answer Douglas hit upon had two parts. First, the land would be divided into two territories, to be called Kansas and Nebraska. Second, the Missouri Compromise would be repealed, or canceled, and the settlers in each territory would decide for themselves whether to allow slavery.

To Douglas, who had few feelings about the rightness or wrongness of slavery, this seemed like a perfect answer. No one expected slavery to take root in Nebraska, for it was too far north. And Kansas—well, no guarantees, but Southerners would have their opportunity to try to make it a slave territory. One for the North, one for the South. What compromise could be fairer?

Unfortunately, Douglas's plan reopened the argument over slavery. Northerners were outraged that this plan would repeal the Missouri Compromise. Southerners were pleased that it did. After an angry debate in Congress, the Kansas-Nebraska Act, as it was called, became law.

Southerners were determined to make Kansas a slave territory. They urged Southerners to move there. Antislavery Northerners were determined that Kansas would be a free territory and urged Northerners to move there. Each group brought guns to Kansas. Before long, the two sides were attacking each other. Two hundred settlers were killed before the U.S. Army moved in to stop the conflict. The territory became known as "Bleeding Kansas."

The struggle over slavery in the nation's western lands had become violent, and no one could say where it would all end.

The Kansas-Nebraska Act: 1854

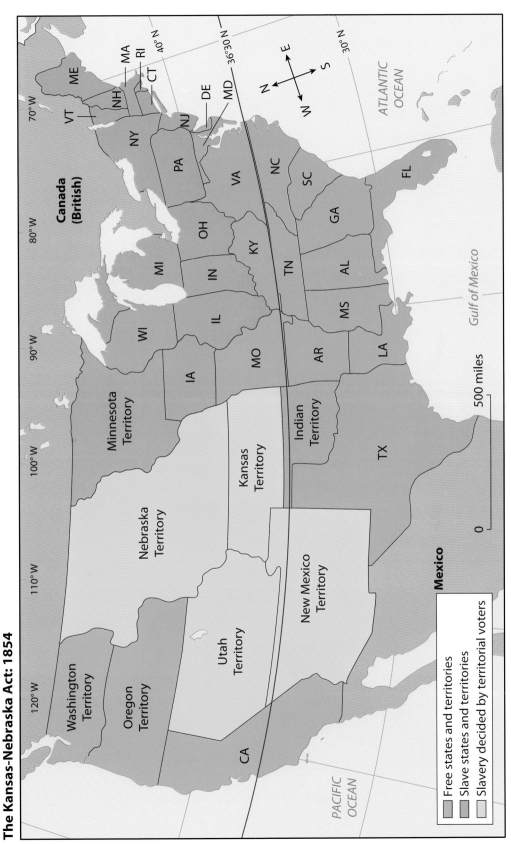

This map illustrates why abolitionists saw the Kansas-Nebraska Act as a threat.

Chapter 7
Young Mr. Lincoln

Lincoln on Slavery Many Northerners opposed to the spread of slavery were attracted to a new political party called the Republican Party. One of the party's leaders was a lawyer from Illinois named Abraham Lincoln.

> **The Big Question**
>
> What shaped Abraham Lincoln as a young man?

For Lincoln, as for a great number of Americans in the North and the West, the question of whether slavery was right or wrong was quite simple. It was just a matter of putting yourself in the other fellow's shoes. "As I would not be a slave, so I would not be a master," he said. "This expresses my idea of democracy. Whatever differs from this . . . is no democracy." Lincoln once said in a private conversation, "Whenever I hear of anyone arguing [in favor of] slavery, I feel a strong impulse to see it tried on him personally."

Although he hated slavery, Lincoln was not an abolitionist. Abolitionists—people such as William Lloyd Garrison, Frederick Douglass, and members of the Underground Railroad—wanted to abolish slavery immediately and everywhere, not just in the territories of the United States but in the Southern states, too.

Abraham Lincoln

They did not care whether the actions against slavery were **constitutional**.

██████████████

Vocabulary

constitutional, adj.
allowed or legal
under the terms of
the U.S. Constitution

Lincoln knew that under the U.S. Constitution, the federal government did not have the right to interfere with slavery in the *states*. The government could, however, stop slavery from entering the territories. If it did that, Lincoln hoped that slavery would gradually die out everywhere in the country. Lincoln cared about ending slavery but wanted to do so constitutionally.

Who Was Abraham Lincoln?

Like so many Americans in the West, Abraham Lincoln started out in life without any special advantages. He was born in a one-room log cabin in Kentucky. His mother could neither read nor write, and his father could barely write his own name.

Abraham's father, Thomas Lincoln, had the unfortunate knack of picking out one piece of bad farmland after another. After struggling to make a living in Kentucky, Thomas moved his family to Indiana, where he again chose land unwisely. Abraham was seven at the time. Like children everywhere on the frontier, he and his sister helped with farm chores. They went to school only when they could be spared from work at home. Altogether, Abraham probably spent less than one year in the schools of Kentucky and Indiana.

He did not miss a great deal, for frontier schools were quite poor. Children of all ages were taught at the same time in the

ABRAHAM LINCOLN'S BIRTHPLACE

Abraham Lincoln was born in this one-room log cabin in Kentucky.

same one-room building. With no books, the children learned by repeating after the teacher. Everyone, at the same time, said their different lessons aloud. It's little wonder that these schools were called "blab schools."

When Abraham was nine years old, tragedy struck the Lincoln home. Abraham's mother died, leaving Thomas to care for his two children alone. A year later, Thomas married again. Abraham's stepmother was a loving person. She taught Abraham to read, and, with her encouragement, he developed a strong desire to learn. The family had only a few books, but Abraham read them over and over. He was willing to travel many miles to borrow books from others. In addition, Abraham took care of all the writing for the Lincoln family. Soon, he was doing the same for many neighbors as well.

Unfortunately, life on the frontier meant there was little time for reading. Always tall and strong for his age, Abraham did more than his share of clearing and plowing the land. His father also hired him out to work for neighbors.

As a teenager, Abraham began to take on jobs away from home. He worked on a ferryboat. He built a flatboat and floated goods down the Mississippi River to New Orleans. He hired himself and a cousin out to split logs into rails for fencing. One spring, the two of them split five thousand logs, a huge amount of work. This earned

Young Abraham Lincoln did all the writing for his family and his neighbors.

Abraham the nickname the "Rail-Splitter." But through these years, Abraham seemed to have no particular goals in life. He later described himself at this time as a piece of floating driftwood.

"Floating driftwood" described the Lincoln family as well. Thomas Lincoln moved the family again when Abraham was nineteen, this time to Illinois. Abraham helped with the usual frontier jobs: building a cabin, clearing and fencing the land, planting crops. A couple of years later, though, when the Lincolns moved yet again, Abraham did not go with them. At twenty-one, he was ready to strike out on his own. He went to live in the small town of New Salem, Illinois.

Lincoln on His Own

Being the newcomer in a small town was uncomfortable at first. Soon after Abraham arrived, the young men of the town challenged him to a wrestling match against their leader, a strong young man named Jack Armstrong. Lincoln, six feet four inches tall and rugged, defeated Armstrong. Immediately after, the two young men became the best of friends, and Lincoln was quickly accepted by all the other young men.

Lincoln did more than wrestle, however. Anxious to improve himself, he joined New Salem's debating club, read more books, and studied grammar and mathematics, all on his own.

After working for a time in a store, Abraham and a partner opened a general store of their own in New Salem. The store did poorly, and when it closed after a year, the two partners owed large debts. When the partner died, Lincoln insisted on paying off all the money himself. It took years, but he paid back every last penny. After that, Lincoln became known as "Honest Abe."

Later, Lincoln studied law and became a lawyer. He moved to nearby Springfield, the capital city of Illinois. Soon, he and a young partner were among the most successful lawyers in town, but few would have guessed that from the look of their office. The windows were never washed. Papers were scattered everywhere and piled high on desks and tables. On one large envelope, Lincoln wrote, "When you can't find it anywhere else, look into this." He often stuffed letters into his tall silk hat. Once when he bought a new hat, he absentmindedly threw out the old one, notes and all.

Lincoln was liked and trusted by his neighbors. They elected him to serve four terms in the Illinois State Legislature. Later he also served one term in the U.S. Congress during the Mexican-American War. After that, Lincoln decided to leave government and go back to his law practice.

But one thing he knew for sure—he was firmly against slavery. And as the slavery issue grew to dominate all other issues in American life, Lincoln knew that he could not remain on the sidelines. He decided he must take an active part in the effort to rid the nation of slavery.

After drifting from job to job as a young man, Abraham Lincoln found his calling and became a successful lawyer.

Chapter 8
The Crisis Deepens

Dred Scott Bleeding Kansas left the nation more divided over the issue of slavery than ever before. Things got even worse in 1857 when the U.S. **Supreme Court** announced its decision in the *Dred Scott* case.

> ### The Big Question
> What led the South to secede?

> **Vocabulary**
>
> **Supreme Court,** n. the highest court in the land

Dred Scott was an African American and a slave in the state of Missouri until he was in his thirties. Then his owner, an army doctor, took him to the state of Illinois, where they lived for several years. The owner also took Dred Scott to the Wisconsin Territory for a time before finally returning to Missouri.

Sometime after, with the help of several antislavery white friends in St. Louis, Dred Scott went to court to seek his freedom. Illinois, said Scott, was a free state where slavery was not allowed. The Wisconsin Territory was above 36° 30' latitude—again, an area where slavery was not allowed. Scott asked the court to rule that as soon as he entered the free state of Illinois and the free Wisconsin Territory, he had automatically become a free man.

Dred Scott

Dred Scott appealed the case all the way to the Supreme Court. The Court, however, decided against him. It was true, said the Court, that no one could own a slave in the free state of Illinois. But once Dred Scott came back to Missouri, he was a slave again.

If that were all the Court said, antislavery people might have grumbled a bit and accepted the decision. But the Court went on to say that a slave was like any other property. And the U.S. Constitution says that Congress cannot take away a person's right to his property by passing a law. Therefore, the law that had prohibited a person from owning slaves in certain territories— that is, the Missouri Compromise—had been unconstitutional all along. In other words, the Missouri Compromise was never a proper law.

Worst of all, the Supreme Court declared that African Americans were not citizens of the United States and could never become citizens. This was a terrible injustice against African Americans, especially the thousands of free African Americans who had been considered citizens and had **exercised** certain civil rights.

Southerners were delighted with this decision. Meanwhile, Northerners were up in arms. If Congress did not have the right to prohibit slavery in a territory, then there was no way to stop the spread of slavery in the territories! Antislavery Northerners made it clear that they would never accept such a situation. The Supreme Court had tried to calm tensions over slavery with the decision. Instead, it ended up making things worse.

The Lincoln-Douglas Debates

The next year, 1858, the people of Illinois prepared to elect a U.S. senator. Stephen A. Douglas, who had already served for many years, ran for reelection. To run against him, the Republicans chose Abraham Lincoln.

In his very first speech after being nominated, Lincoln summed up the situation facing the nation as he saw it. "A house divided against itself cannot stand," said Lincoln. "I believe this government cannot **endure** permanently half *slave* and half *free*. I do not expect the Union to be ***dissolved***—I do not expect the house to *fall*—but I *do* expect it will cease to be divided. It will become *all* one thing, or *all* the other." Lincoln said that if the spread of slavery was not stopped now and made to disappear, then it would spread all through the nation. "It will become *all* one thing, or *all* the other."

Lincoln's debates with Stephen Douglas brought him national attention.

In seven cities up and down the state, Lincoln and Douglas debated each other before crowds of thousands. Lincoln said that he believed African Americans were "entitled to all the **natural rights** . . . in the Declaration of Independence," including the right to liberty. In these rights, Lincoln said, African Americans were *"my equal and the equal of Judge Douglas, and the equal of every living man."* Stephen A. Douglas disagreed. Douglas believed that African Americans had no such rights. They were in no way his equal.

Lincoln went on to ask: Now that the Supreme Court ruled that Congress couldn't keep slavery out of the territories, was there any way to stop the spread of slavery? If not, wouldn't slavery continue to spread?

Not necessarily, replied Douglas. That was up to the people in each new territory. If they did not want slavery, then they wouldn't permit it.

Newspapers all over the country reported the words of these two candidates. When the votes were counted, Douglas won the election. But the campaign made Abraham Lincoln a well-known figure throughout America.

John Brown

The U.S. government had built an **arsenal** in Harpers Ferry, a small town nestled in the foothills of the Appalachian Mountains in western Virginia (now West Virginia). A quiet town, Harpers Ferry was not prepared for the fame that was about to come to it.

In the dark hours of October 16, 1859, a band of nineteen men crossed the Potomac River from Maryland. The men took the arsenal by surprise and captured it. The mayor of the town and two others were killed in the attack.

Abolitionist John Brown led the attack. Brown believed he had been chosen by God to end slavery. He and his five sons had lived in Kansas. There, they had killed five Southern settlers during the days of bleeding Kansas.

To some abolitionists, this made Brown a hero. When he told some wealthy abolitionists in New York State that he had a plan to strike a major blow against slavery, they provided him with money. Brown's plan, which he did not reveal to the New Yorkers, was to seize the arsenal at Harpers Ferry and give the arms to nearby slaves. The slaves would then rise up in rebellion, kill their masters, and create a free area in the mountains of Maryland and Virginia. From there, the newly freed slaves would encourage slave rebellions throughout the South.

The plan never had a chance of succeeding. Brown himself was so disorganized that he forgot to bring food for his men. Many of his men were killed in a shootout with the townspeople of Harpers Ferry. Within a day after the attack, U.S. Marines under the command of Robert E. Lee cornered Brown and his men in a building. When Brown refused to surrender, they stormed the building and captured Brown and seven others.

Brown was quickly tried by the state of Virginia, found guilty, and hanged. His raid drove the North and the South even further apart. In the North, many newspapers and leaders, such as Lincoln, spoke out against Brown's violence.

U.S. Marines captured John Brown after Brown's attack at Harpers Ferry.

Some leading abolitionists, however, called him a hero and even agreed with his methods to end slavery. In the South, Brown's raid reawakened the nightmare of slave revolts. Those who wanted to secede from the Union now could say to their fellow Southerners, "Do you see what the North wants to do to us? And this is only the beginning. We must leave the Union now!"

The Election of 1860

As the election of 1860 drew near, it was clear to all Americans that it might be the most important election in the young nation's history. Quite possibly, it might be the last one.

The Republican Party chose Abraham Lincoln as its candidate for president of the United States. Lincoln and the Republicans guaranteed slavery wherever it then existed and condemned John Brown, but they also promised to do everything they could to keep slavery out of the territories. But the South did not trust the Republicans, or Abraham Lincoln. No matter how many times they promised not to interfere with slavery in the Southern states where it already existed, the South did not believe them. Several Southern states said that if a Republican was elected president, they would secede.

And that is exactly what happened. In November 1860, Abraham Lincoln was elected president. One month later, South Carolina seceded from the Union. Over the next six weeks, Mississippi, Florida, Alabama, Georgia, Louisiana, and Texas also voted to leave.

At that moment the future of the United States of America looked grim. In fact, it was not clear that the United States had any future at all.

Abraham Lincoln was sworn in as president in March 1861. This means he took the oath of office.

Chapter 9
The War Begins

Secession Events moved swiftly. Abraham Lincoln's term as president did not officially start until March 4, 1861. One month before then, on February 4, representatives from the seven seceding states met in Montgomery, Alabama.

The Big Question

Why did the attack on Fort Sumter launch the American Civil War?

Three days later, the seceding states announced the creation of a new nation, the **Confederate** States of America. The new nation was called the Confederacy for short. The Confederacy adopted a constitution guaranteeing the future of slavery. Then the representatives from the seven seceding states chose Jefferson Davis, a cotton planter and slave owner from Mississippi, as the first president of the Confederate States of America. Davis had fought bravely in the Mexican-American War and had also served in Congress as a U.S. senator.

Even before the new Confederate States of America was declared, each of the states that seceded had begun to take over forts, arsenals,

Jefferson Davis

post offices, and other U.S. government property in their states. They believed the property belonged to them because the United States no longer had any rights within the Confederate States. By the time Lincoln took over as president, only two forts in the seven Confederate States remained under the control of the United States.

President Lincoln faced a massive problem as he began his term of office. Seven Southern states had already left the Union. Eight other slave states remained in the Union, but four of them had already warned Lincoln: if you use force against the seven states that seceded, we will join them. That would make the new Confederate States of America bigger and stronger. Yet Lincoln knew that if he did not use force, he could not make the seceding states return to the Union.

Lincoln decided to make one last appeal to the Southern states that had seceded. At the start of each new term of office, presidents take an oath of office and then deliver a speech, called the inaugural address. Lincoln used his inaugural address to appeal to the South to stay in the Union. He reassured the South, as he had done before, that he did not intend "to interfere with . . . slavery in the States where it exists. I believe I have no lawful right to do so, and I have no inclination [desire] to do so."

When it came to secession, however, Lincoln said that he had no choice. As president he had a duty to **preserve** the Union, to enforce its laws, and to protect its property.

But, Lincoln told the South, "there will be no invasion, no using of force against or among the people anywhere." And he urged the

The Union and the Confederacy, 1861

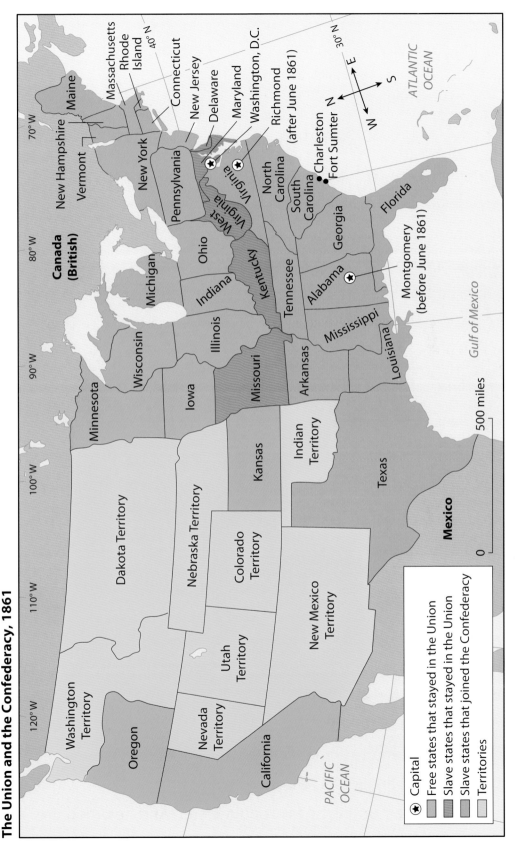

In response to Lincoln's election as president, many slave states seceded and formed the Confederate States of America.

South not to do anything hasty. "We are not enemies, but friends," said Lincoln in closing. "We must not be enemies."

Too Late for Words

The president's carefully chosen words changed nothing. It was too late for words. In South Carolina, events marched toward a showdown. One of the two Southern forts that the U.S. government still controlled was located on an island in the harbor of Charleston, South Carolina. This was Fort Sumter. Earlier, South Carolina had demanded that the fort be handed over along with all the others. Major Robert Anderson, in charge of the fort, refused.

But now Fort Sumter was running short on supplies. Major Anderson told the president that unless food arrived soon, he would have to give up.

The only way to get supplies to Fort Sumter was by ship. The ships would have to pass in front of the guns of the Confederate States located on other islands in the harbor. President Lincoln wanted to send the needed supplies, but he didn't want to start a war over them. He informed South Carolina that the ships he was sending to Fort Sumter carried only food and supplies—no fresh soldiers, no guns, no **ammunition**. Surely, he believed, there would be no reason to fire on the ships. President Jefferson Davis of the Confederacy decided otherwise.

If supplies reached the fort, Anderson and his men could continue to hold out. Davis would not allow that. Before the supply ships could arrive, he instructed

> **Vocabulary**
>
> **ammunition**, n.
> bullets or shells

The Confederate bombardment of Fort Sumter meant that the American Civil War had begun.

the local commander to demand the fort's surrender. When Major Anderson refused, Confederate cannons on shore opened fire. After thirty hours of shelling, Major Anderson surrendered.

That did it. Confederate guns had fired upon the forces of the United States of America. In the eyes of the Confederacy, its gunners had struck a blow for Confederate independence. In the eyes of the Union, they had started a rebellion. Soon after, Lincoln called for Americans to join the army to put down the rebellion. Of course, that was the very action those other four Southern states had warned against—using force against the seceding states. Now those states, too—Arkansas, Virginia, North Carolina, and Tennessee—withdrew from the Union and joined the Confederacy. The war had begun.

Chapter 10
Advantages and Disadvantages

Summer Picnic A holiday mood filled the air on July 21, 1861, as people climbed into their carriages to ride from Washington, D.C., into the Virginia countryside. They were heading for Manassas Junction, about thirty miles away. There, they planned to have lunch while watching the first battle of the Civil War.

The Big Question

What resources and advantages did each side have at the start of the Civil War?

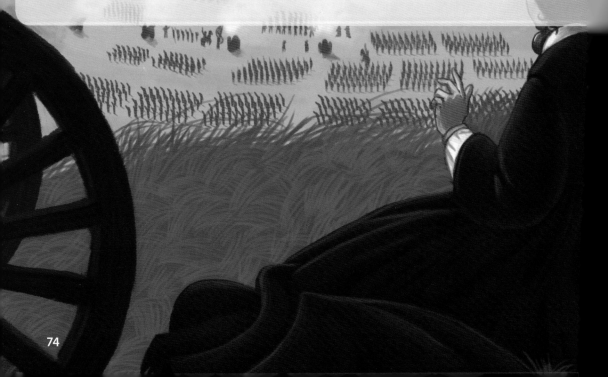

People traveled to watch the first battle between the North and the South. No one expected a lengthy war.

Five days earlier, about thirty-five thousand Union troops marched out of the nation's capital shouting, "Forward to Richmond!" Richmond, Virginia, was the capital of the new Confederate States of America, and the Union army wanted to capture it. After several days the Union soldiers reached Manassas Junction. A Confederate force of twenty-five thousand was there to meet them. Newspapers in Washington reported that a battle was expected to begin shortly. This was the battle the people had come to watch.

A few miles away, near a small stream called Bull Run, the fighting had already started. People could hear the roar of cannons and the crackle of gunfire in the distance.

'Good, we're on time for the show,' the spectators thought. They were anxious not to miss this first battle of the war, for it might well be the last one. At least, that's what most people in the North were saying. The Union army would take the field, defeat the rebels quickly, and go on to capture Richmond. The Southern states would then return to the Union, and the war would be over.

Many Southerners also expected the war to end quickly, but with a different result. As one Georgia woman later remembered, "We had an idea that when our soldiers got upon the ground and showed unmistakably that they were really ready and willing to fight . . . the whole trouble would be declared at an end."

Both sets of expectations were wrong. The **tide of battle** that day went back and forth, with neither side able to get the upper hand at first. Except for the top officers, most soldiers on each side were untrained, disorganized, and confused. They were also amazingly brave.

Late in the afternoon it appeared that the Union forces might be winning. Then 32,300 fresh Confederate troops arrived by train and quickly entered the battle. That was enough to turn the tide. The half-trained Union soldiers began to retreat—first a few, then more and more, until finally thousands dropped their guns and ran in panic toward the picnickers.

The First Battle of Bull Run did not go as expected. The South was not going to retreat and give up.

Now, frightened sightseers scrambled back to their carriages. They were joined on the road by the fleeing soldiers, some of them wounded, some just tired, and all of them frightened. For hours, the road to Washington was clogged. Fortunately for the Union side, the Confederate generals decided that their own troops were too tired to pursue the Union soldiers.

Watching the men straggling back to the capital the next day, a British journalist wrote: "I saw a steady stream of men covered with mud, soaked through with rain. . . . [I asked] a pale young man who looked exhausted to death . . . where the men were coming from. 'Where from? Well, sir, I guess we're all coming out of Virginny as fast as we can, and pretty well whipped too. . . . I know I'm going home. I've had enough of fighting to last my lifetime.'"

After the First Battle of Bull Run, the hard truth began to sink in. This war would not end quickly after all. It would probably be long and bloody.

How would the war end? No one could say. But the North did have many advantages. The North's population was about twice as large as the South's total population. However, as the South had no intention of giving guns to slaves, the North actually had four times as many men who could fight on the battlefields. With its mills and factories, the North could produce twenty times as much iron, twenty-five times as much railroad equipment, and thirty times as many guns as the South. With other factories producing all the clothing, blankets, tents, and medical supplies needed by the Union armies, the North didn't have to rely on European countries for these goods, as the South did. And with many more miles of railroad track, the North could move its troops and supplies more easily than the South.

Is Bigger Better?

There is more to winning a war than having such advantages as the North, however. Remember the American Revolution? Great Britain had a far larger population. It had a bigger and better trained army. It had a larger navy. It had far more weapons than the American Patriots. But it still lost the war. Would this happen to the North as well?

At the start of the Civil War, both sides had plenty of men and supplies. The North's larger population and factory production would be a big advantage only if the war dragged on for a number of years. That's when Confederate armies would feel the pinch of not having enough men to replace those killed and wounded. That's when they would find themselves short of supplies. But if the Confederate army could win enough early battles, Northerners might lose heart and quit the war before their advantages really mattered.

The Confederacy had its own advantages, too. The biggest was that it was fighting a **defensive** war. The South did not have to conquer an inch of Northern land to win. All it had to do was successfully defend its own land against Northern armies. Knowing that they were fighting to defend their own land and homes gave Southern soldiers an extra reason to fight hard.

> **Vocabulary**
>
> **defensive,** adj. designed to keep safe or protect against attack

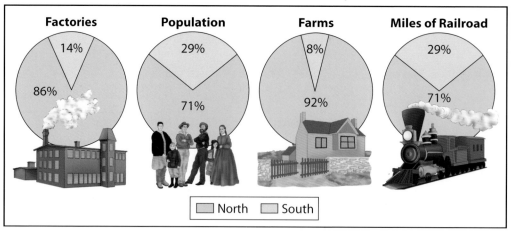

Union and Confederate Resources, 1860

Factories	Population	Farms	Miles of Railroad
14% / 86%	29% / 71%	8% / 92%	29% / 71%

North ▢ South ▢

The North had many advantages that would help it survive a long war. The South also had advantages—ones that could not be easily measured.

Another benefit for the South came in the form of one man— an outstanding general by the name of Robert E. Lee. In fact President Lincoln asked Lee to take charge of all the Union armies. But Lee, like so many others of that time, felt a deep attachment to his home state of Virginia. In fact, many people at that time referred to their home state as their "country." As it was just a matter of time before Virginia joined the Confederacy, Lee refused President Lincoln's offer, explaining, "If I owned four million slaves, I would cheerfully give them up to save the Union. But to lift my hand against Virginia is impossible. . . . [I cannot] fight against my relatives, my children, my home."

Instead, Lee chose to be a general in the Confederate army. Lee proved to be a great general and was deeply respected by his men. Although his armies were usually outnumbered, General Lee used daring surprise moves to win many victories. Although it took a little longer, able generals emerged for the Union side also.

As the war went on, General Lee could not turn against his fellow Virginians and instead led the Confederate Army.

Chapter 11
Developing a Strategy

The Scott Plan General Winfield Scott had known all along that this war would not be ended with one quick, decisive battle. The First Battle of Bull Run proved him right. Scott knew war. He had fought in every American war since the War of 1812.

> **The Big Question**
>
> What was General Winfield Scott's plan to win the war, and how successful was it?

A hero of the war with Mexico, General Winfield Scott was an experienced military leader.

In the war with Mexico, it was Scott who led American troops in triumph into Mexico City. After an unsuccessful run for the presidency in 1852, Scott returned to his duties as commanding general of all American forces.

A native Virginian who opposed slavery, Scott remained with the Union. This was unlike some of his fellow Virginians, such as Lee, who sided with the Confederacy. At age seventy-five, General Scott could no longer command troops in the field. However, he could still use his experience to develop a winning **strategy** for the war. He got to work right after Fort Sumter fell.

Scott explained his plan to President Lincoln: The Appalachian Mountains and the Mississippi River divided the Confederacy into three nearly equal parts. The Confederacy could be weakened by isolating each of those parts. The first step would be to gain control of the Mississippi River and the three Confederate states on the western side of the river—Texas, Arkansas, and Louisiana. This action would cut off those states from the rest of the Confederacy. They would be knocked out of the war.

> **Vocabulary**
>
> **strategy,** n. a plan of action created to achieve a specific goal
>
> **blockade,** n. a military strategy aimed at preventing people and goods from entering or leaving an area

At the same time, the navy would be used to set up a naval **blockade**. A blockade would prevent ships from entering or leaving the Confederacy's ports on the Atlantic and Gulf coasts.

The Confederacy would be unable to sell its cotton to Europe or buy the supplies it needed. Therefore, as the Confederacy grew

Scott's Strategy

Scott's plan to win the war was to pressure the Confederacy on every side.

weaker, the Union would press its advantage in **manpower** and supplies. By then, the Union's large armies would be experienced in battle. They would be ready to advance from the north and from the west, cutting the Confederacy into still smaller parts and defeating them.

Vocabulary

manpower, n. the number of people available for a task

President Lincoln came to recognize that Scott's strategy was a sound one. Others, however, criticized it for being too slow and too timid. They ridiculed Scott's plan, calling it the "anaconda strategy." An anaconda is a long snake that kills by wrapping itself around its prey and slowly crushing it. The critics called for a bold plan that would end the war in months, not years. Even President Lincoln worried that the nation might grow weary of a long war. Lincoln supported an early battle to settle the issue.

But Scott knew that the Confederate armies were not going to crumble after a few battles. They had too many fine leaders and too many brave men. The Union could win, but only after a long, hard fight. The First Battle of Bull Run proved him right.

The day after Fort Sumter surrendered, President Lincoln declared a naval blockade. However, in the early years of the war, the blockade was not effective. No ship can be everywhere at once, and the Union had only forty-two ships to patrol a shoreline of 3,500 miles and 189 ports. During 1861, nine out of every ten ships that tried to "run" the blockade made it safely. By the start of 1862, Northern shipyards began to produce large numbers of warships, and the Union's navy was more successful. By the end of the war, the Union navy numbered seven hundred vessels, and the blockade was far more effective.

The *Virginia* and the *Monitor*

For a short time in early 1862, it looked like the South might have a weapon that could shatter the Union blockade. Back at the start of the war, the U.S. Navy had to leave its base in Norfolk, Virginia, because Confederate forces were closing in. As the Union warships hurried out of port, one of them, the *Merrimack*, caught fire and sank in shallow waters. Later the Confederates raised the ship, cut off its burned top, and covered its sides with a double layer of two-inch-thick iron plates. Each side had holes for five large naval guns. On its bow (the front of the ship) was a 1,500-pound iron battering ram.

All this work took many months, but on March 8, 1862, the ironclad ship, now renamed the *Virginia*, steamed out of Norfolk's harbor and took on two large Union warships. Cannonballs simply bounced off the *Virginia*'s slanted sides and fell harmlessly into the water. The *Virginia* sank both Union ships and scattered several others before anchoring for the night.

The Union navy, however, had been building its own ironclad ship, called the *Monitor*. The next day, as the *Virginia* steamed out to destroy more Union ships, the *Monitor* was waiting for it. For four hours, a battle raged as hundreds watched from the shore. Although each side claimed victory, neither ship could sink the other.

Neither side won a clear victory in this battle between ironclad ships.

For the next two months, though, fearful of the *Virginia*, Union ships steered clear of the waters off Norfolk. Then in May, as Union troops advanced on Norfolk, it was the Confederacy's turn to abandon the port. Rather than allow the *Virginia* to fall into the Union's hands, Confederate soldiers destroyed the ship. The Confederacy unsuccessfully tried to buy other ironclad warships from European countries. Without such ships, the Confederacy had no chance of breaking the Union's blockade.

Mississippi River Ports

In 1862, Union warships commanded by Captain David Farragut made a bold move to carry out a second part of Scott's strategy. Their goal was to cut off Texas, Arkansas, and Louisiana from the rest of the Confederacy. Farragut was the commander of a fleet of twenty-three warships blockading the mouth of the Mississippi River. New Orleans, by far the Confederacy's biggest port, was just a short way upriver. Farragut believed that if he could take the enemy by surprise, he could capture the city. After his ships bombarded Confederate forts near the mouth of the river for five days, Farragut ordered his fleet upstream. Despite heavy fire, he captured New Orleans. Confederate ships could still sail down the Mississippi River. But they could no longer use the port at its mouth to unload goods, and they could not get to the open sea.

Meanwhile, Union armies, led by General Ulysses S. Grant, fought fierce battles in the South. By the end of 1862, Grant had won several victories. But at Shiloh, near the Mississippi border,

Union Captain David Farragut captured New Orleans and prevented Confederate ships from using its port.

a Confederate army caught Grant by surprise. The resulting battle lasted for two days. Both sides suffered heavy loss of life. In the end, however, Grant drove the Confederate troops back.

So, by the end of 1862, this is how matters stood in the West: Union forces had won control of most of the Mississippi River. Confederate troops, though, still held several important ports, including Vicksburg, Mississippi. This allowed the states of Arkansas, Texas, and Louisiana to continue helping the Confederacy by sending men and supplies across the great river. Until Union forces could take those river ports, the anaconda would not be able to tighten its grip on the South.

Chapter 12
The War in the East

On to Richmond In the East the Union was far less successful. There, the Union's main goal was to capture the Confederacy's capital city, Richmond, Virginia.

The Big Question

What prompted Lincoln to remove General McClellan from command?

Capturing the enemy's capital is often an important goal in war. It disrupts their government and can cause their people to lose heart. For the same reason, the Union side always rushed troops to defend its own capital, Washington, D.C., whenever it seemed like Confederate armies might attack it. In the case of Richmond, though, the Union would also be capturing much more than a capital city. The Confederacy's most important railroad center, its largest iron mill, and its largest maker of guns were in Richmond. If the Union took Richmond, the Confederacy might collapse then and there.

Three days after the defeat at Bull Run, President Lincoln changed generals. He appointed George B. McClellan to command the eastern army, which came to be called the Army of the Potomac.

George B. McClellan

George McClellan was only thirty-four years old, very young for such great responsibility. However, he was known as a brilliant organizer. And that is exactly what this collection of untrained **volunteers** needed if it was to become an effective army. Unfortunately, he could be arrogant, and slow to attack the enemy.

To help McClellan train his men, Lincoln gave the general his full support. When McClellan asked for more money and supplies, he got them. When he asked for more men, he got those, too. Eventually, McClellan had 110,000 men under his command. He had one of the largest armies ever gathered. By the end of 1861, he was writing to his wife that he expected to "crush the rebels in one campaign."

As weeks stretched into months, President Lincoln wondered just when that campaign might take place. December and January came and went with no action. In mid-February, McClellan wrote, "In ten days I shall be in Richmond." But still his troops had not moved. Even a message from the president telling him, "you must act," didn't get McClellan to move.

It was now clear that McClellan was all talk. In reality, he had little stomach for fighting. His great weakness was his **caution**. Every time he seemed ready to move, something caused him to rethink and delay moving his troops.

Usually that something was a report—always inaccurate—that the enemy had more troops. Convinced he would be outnumbered, McClellan would ask for additional troops. Lincoln's **secretary of war** once said, "If [McClellan] had a million men, he would swear the enemy had two million, and then he would sit down in the mud and yell for three." President Lincoln grew so frustrated that he remarked, "If General McClellan does not want to use the army I would like to *borrow* it."

Some of General McClellan's officers in Virginia in 1863.

The Peninsula Campaign

Finally, even McClellan was ready to move from his training base near Washington. Lincoln thought McClellan should march directly to Richmond. Confederate armies were ready to defend that route, however, so McClellan offered a different plan. He would take most of the Army of the Potomac by boat to the Virginia **Peninsula**, which lies between the York and James rivers. This would be a huge task of organization, but it was exactly the kind of thing McClellan was good at. The army would then move north up the peninsula toward Richmond, attacking it from behind. A second Union army would march south from Washington to keep Confederate troops along that route busy. The two armies would then meet and take Richmond.

It was a good plan, but to succeed, it would take daring, **decisiveness**, and speed. None of these three things were McClellan's strong points. The first part went smoothly. In late March, McClellan floated his army of 110,000 down the Potomac River. More than one hundred Union boats landed near the tip of the peninsula. But then, McClellan spent endless days organizing and reorganizing and retraining his troops. When he finally started north, he moved slowly and cautiously, even though there were few Confederate troops on the peninsula. Along the way, he spent a whole month trying to capture a small Confederate force at Yorktown.

> **Vocabulary**
>
> **peninsula,** adj. of or related to a piece of land that sticks out into a body of water
>
> **decisiveness,** n. an ability to make decisions quickly

Confederate generals knew how to use this time. They moved their troops into position to fight against the Union army moving up the peninsula. Meanwhile, Stonewall Jackson raced his troops through the nearby Shenandoah Valley. There, he kept about forty thousand Union troops busy. And what about the Union general whose army was

Stonewall Jackson (center) was a highly skilled general who fought in many major battles.

to join McClellan at Richmond? With Stonewall Jackson on the loose so near the capital, he decided to stay put and defend Washington instead.

Meanwhile, McClellan slowly moved forward. By the end of May, his army was just six miles from Richmond, close enough to see the spires of its churches and to hear the ringing of church bells. That was as far as they got.

On May 31, a Confederate force struck the Army of the Potomac hard, stopping it in its tracks. Several weeks later, Robert E. Lee and Stonewall Jackson hit hard again in battles that lasted for seven days. Both sides suffered heavy losses in the Seven Days' Battle, but Union armies were driven away from Richmond.

Lincoln and his military advisers now decided that McClellan's peninsula campaign, as it was called, could not succeed. The president ordered McClellan to return to Washington.

A year and a half after the seceding states formed the Confederate States of America, and a year after the first big battle at Bull Run, Union armies in the East had nothing to show for their efforts, and the South was more confident than ever that it could never be conquered.

Antietam

Over the next few months, General Lee's forces were particularly successful in Virginia and, in particular, at the Second Battle of Bull Run. Then, in September 1862, Lee carried the war into the United States. He sent his troops across the Potomac River into Maryland, one of the slave states that had remained in the Union. A lot of Marylanders believed in the Confederate cause. If Lee could defeat the Union army there, then perhaps Maryland would join the Confederacy.

Lee planned to go even farther north, into Pennsylvania. If he could take Harrisburg, the state's capital, he would destroy the North's railroad lines, cutting off the eastern cities from the West. He could also get food and much needed supplies, especially shoes, for his troops. Victories in Maryland and Pennsylvania might cause the North to lose heart and quit the war.

Lee might have succeeded, if he hadn't had some very bad luck. A Union soldier came upon a campsite recently used by

Confederate troops, where he spotted a small bundle of cigars wrapped in paper. When the soldier unwrapped the bundle and saw what was written on the paper, his eyes must have opened wide. The paper, which was rushed to the headquarters of General McClellan, revealed General Lee's battle plans. Lee had divided his army, sending Stonewall Jackson's men on another mission. After Jackson completed that mission, he was supposed to join Lee.

McClellan now knew exactly where the enemy would be. He knew he would be able to hit Lee's smaller force before Jackson could return. "Here is a piece of paper," McClellan stated confidently, "with which if I cannot whip Bobby Lee, I will be willing to go home."

Alas for the Union, however, McClellan was still McClellan—too cautious, too worried about the enemy's strength, and always finding reasons for delay. By the time he finally moved, most of Jackson's forces had returned to join Lee.

On September 17, 1862, the two sides met in battle at Antietam Creek, also known as the Battle of Sharpsburg. The Union usually named battles for nearby natural features such as creeks, rivers, and mountains; the Confederates named battles for the closest towns. That's why the North called the first battle of the war Bull Run (a run is a rapidly running stream), while the South called it Manassas.

The fighting at Antietam Creek was fierce. First one side seemed to get the upper hand, then the other. Late in the day, Union forces were making progress, when the rest of Jackson's troops arrived in time to turn them back.

General McClellan failed to press his advantage at the Battle of Antietam.

At the end of the day, neither side had defeated the other. But Lee had held nothing back. He had used all of his men in battle, and now they were exhausted and short of supplies. McClellan still had twenty thousand fresh troops. Had McClellan attacked the next day, he might have finished off Lee's army. Instead, McClellan held back, which allowed the Confederate troops to cross the Potomac River and get back to Virginia.

President Lincoln was fit to be tied. He took a train to Sharpsburg and *ordered* McClellan to go after Lee. "I came back thinking he would move at once," Lincoln later wrote. "It was nineteen days before he put a man over the [Potomac] river, nine days longer before he got his army across"—remember, Lee had gotten his army across in one day!—"and then he stopped again."

That was the end for Lincoln. He removed McClellan from command and assigned the general to sign up volunteers for the army in Trenton, New Jersey. McClellan never held another command.

Antietam was the bloodiest day of the entire Civil War, as well as the bloodiest single day in U.S. history. Altogether, 23,000 Union and Confederate soldiers were lost on that one awful day. President Lincoln had hoped for a clear and decisive victory, and not just for military reasons. He planned to make an important announcement—the most important announcement of the entire war, as you will soon read. He believed the best time to do this would be after a Union victory.

Was Antietam enough of a victory? The Union had stopped Lee's drive into the North. Certainly that was a big plus. On the other hand, the South didn't need to conquer Northern land to win. All it had to do was keep from getting conquered itself. And thanks to McClellan's caution, Lee's army had survived to fight another day.

Perhaps Antietam was not the great victory Lincoln had hoped for, but it would have to do.

After the battle at Antietam, President Lincoln fired General McClellan.

Chapter 13
The Emancipation Proclamation

Forever Free When the Civil War began, Lincoln said that the goal of the war would be to preserve the Union—not to end slavery. Indeed the preservation and love of the Union was the reason that millions of Northerners were willing to fight against their fellow countrymen in the South.

> **The Big Question**
>
> How did the Emancipation Proclamation change the focus of the war effort from the Union point of view?

It is true to say that Lincoln hated slavery. But he did not state that the reason for civil war was to destroy slavery. Why was that? Lincoln had several reasons. Four slave states—Missouri, Kentucky, Maryland, and Delaware—had so far stayed in the Union. They came to be called the border states, because they were located on the border of the North and the South. If they believed the Union's goal was to end slavery, they would almost certainly join the Confederacy. That would mean their population and resources would leave the Union and become a part of the Confederacy. Furthermore, Union armies would have to conquer that much more land to win the war. Lincoln also knew that the millions of Democrats and some conservative Republicans in the loyal states

The Union had to defend Washington, D.C., at all costs.

would only support a war to restore the Union—not one to achieve **emancipation**.

Vocabulary

emancipation, n. the act of setting someone or something free

Keeping Kentucky and Maryland on the Union side was especially important. Lincoln once said, "I think to lose Kentucky is nearly the same as to lose the whole game." In other words, the Union would lose the war. Losing Maryland posed a different problem. If Maryland joined Virginia in the Confederacy, Washington, D.C., the capital city of the Union, would be completely surrounded by Confederate states.

Lincoln had another reason for saying that the Union's goal was only to preserve the Union. Most Northerners agreed that saving the Union was worth a war. They did not necessarily agree that freeing the slaves was worth a war. Being against slavery was one thing; being willing to go to war to end it was another. Abolitionists, of course, believed that ending slavery was exactly what the war should be about. However, Lincoln knew he must wait for more Northerners to agree with the abolitionists. Otherwise, he would risk losing support for the war.

By the summer of 1862, President Lincoln felt that the time was right to announce a change in the Union's goals for the war. This would be a change he hoped would defeat the Confederacy. "The moment came when I felt that slavery must die that the nation might live," said Lincoln. That summer he stayed up late writing and rewriting a document called the Emancipation Proclamation. He would announce that as of January 1, 1863, all slaves in states still rebelling against the United States would be "forever free."

The Emancipation Proclamation was ready in July 1862. Unfortunately, that was right after Union armies had suffered a series of defeats. Lincoln's secretary of state, William Seward, advised him, "Wait until the Union wins an important victory." Otherwise, announcing the proclamation then would look like a desperate effort to escape defeat at the hands of the Confederacy. Lincoln waited. Antietam was not quite the victory Lincoln had hoped for, but he decided it was good enough.

President Lincoln had also carefully considered his constitutional authority over slavery. In his inaugural address he had promised the South that he had no authority over slavery and could not interfere

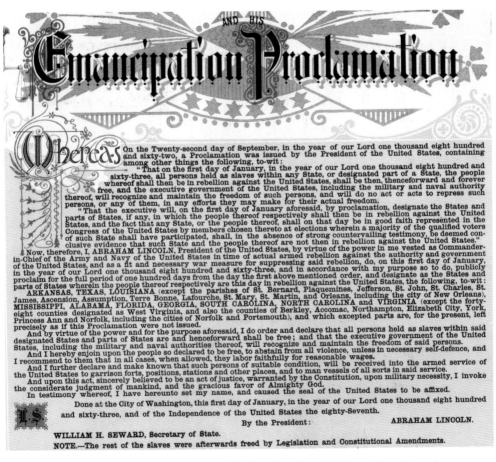

In the Emancipation Proclamation, Lincoln freed enslaved African Americans in Confederate states.

with it before the war started. However, now that he was the Commander in Chief of a nation at war, he could use his wartime powers to hurt the Confederate war effort by freeing the slaves.

On September 22, 1862, five days after Antietam, Lincoln issued his preliminary Emancipation Proclamation. In it he stated that if the rebels did not rejoin the Union by January 1863, all slaves in the rebellious states would be set free. When the Confederacy did not act, President Lincoln signed the final Emancipation Proclamation on January 1, 1863.

The Beginning of Freedom

It's important to understand what the Emancipation Proclamation was and what it wasn't. It did not free any slaves in the border states because these states were not rebelling against the United States. Nor did it free any slaves in areas controlled by the U.S. Army. If Lincoln had done that, at least three border states would immediately have left the Union. That would seriously weaken the Union's chances of winning the war, and then maybe *no* slaves would be free. The proclamation freed only the slaves in the eleven Confederate states that were still rebelling against the United States. If the Confederates actually stopped fighting and ended the war before January 1, they could keep their slaves. Until Union armies entered those states, however, Lincoln could say what he wanted, but he couldn't actually free a single slave.

That's why some people said the Emancipation Proclamation didn't really mean very much. But these people missed the point. After the proclamation, as long as the Union won the war, slavery was finished. Slaves understood the importance of the proclamation. News of it spread through slave quarters all across the South. The proclamation was the beginning of an answer to their prayers for freedom. In the North, the abolitionist and former slave Frederick Douglass wrote, "We shout for joy that we live to record this **righteous decree**."

On the other hand, Lincoln knew that his emergency war powers would not last after the war. He needed a constitutional amendment to make the Emancipation Proclamation and the end of slavery permanent in the United States.

The Emancipation Proclamation was the most important American document about freedom since the Declaration of Independence in 1776. It was a step toward fulfilling the declaration's promise that all people should have the right to "life, liberty, and the pursuit of happiness."

New Year's Day, January 1, 1863, Lincoln signed the Emancipation Proclamation. As he did, he said, "I never, in my life, felt more certain that I was doing right than in signing this paper."

This painting by William Tolman Carlton is called *The Hour of Emancipation*.

Chapter 14
The Generals

Three Leading Generals The three most important generals during the Civil War were Robert E. Lee and Thomas J. "Stonewall" Jackson for the Confederacy, and Ulysses S. Grant for the Union.

The Big Question

How were the three great Civil War generals alike and different?

Robert E. Lee

Robert E. Lee came from a family of patriots and military leaders. His father was the Revolutionary War hero Henry "Light-Horse Harry" Lee. Robert E. Lee himself was married to the great-granddaughter of George Washington's wife, Martha. After finishing first in his class at West Point Military Academy, Robert E. Lee served brilliantly in the Mexican-American War.

At the start of the Civil War, Lee was fifty-four years old and a **colonel** in the U.S. Army. Deciding to fight for the Confederacy instead of the Union was a difficult choice for him.

Vocabulary

colonel, n. a high-ranking military official

Robert E. Lee

Ulysses S. Grant

Lee quickly became known for his daring strategies. For example, every student at West Point learned that a commander does not divide his army. If an army is divided, the enemy can pour troops between the two parts, keep them from rejoining, and then defeat one part at a time. Yet Lee did that several times and got away with it.

Military experts also warned against going into battle with many fewer troops than the enemy. But there were times when Lee had to do just that. Usually, he came out the winner.

Lee was kind to his fellow officers and his men. He inspired confidence, and his troops were devoted to him.

Stonewall Jackson

The second great Confederate general was Lee's partner and right-hand man, Thomas J. "Stonewall" Jackson. Jackson got his nickname in the first battle of the war at Bull Run. As Confederate troops led by Jackson held firm against a Union attack, a Southern officer shouted, "There is Jackson standing like a stone wall." The men cheered, and ever afterward the general was known as Stonewall Jackson.

"Stonewall" was a catchy nickname, but it did not describe Jackson well at all. A stone wall stands firmly in one place and is always on the defensive. Jackson, as a general, was always on the move and nearly always on the attack. Jackson described his ideas on warfare: "Always **mystify**, mislead, and

> **Vocabulary**
>
> **mystify,** v. to confuse

surprise the enemy. And when you strike and overcome him never let up in the pursuit."

Thomas J. "Stonewall" Jackson

Like so many other generals who served the Confederacy, Stonewall Jackson had gone to West Point and later fought in the Mexican-American War. In the nine years before the Civil War, he was a professor of mathematics and science at the Virginia Military Institute. Students remembered him as a quiet man who went about his own business. What they didn't know was that during all those years, Jackson was also studying the strategy and **tactics** of war on his own. When war came, he knew more about strategy and tactics than anyone else on either side.

Vocabulary

tactic, n. an action used to reach a goal

In war, being able to move forces quickly is often the key to success. No one did that better than Stonewall Jackson. He was the opposite of the cautious George B. McClellan. He would be many miles away, and the enemy would be sure he could not get to the battlefield in time to affect the outcome. But suddenly, there they were, Jackson and his troops, pitching in and swinging the tide of battle in the Confederacy's favor. Once, Jackson moved a brigade—a force smaller than an army but still a large group—four hundred miles in a month. That's nearly

General Stonewall Jackson often prayed with his soldiers before a battle.

fifteen miles a day, every day, with soldiers carrying fifty to sixty pound packs on their backs.

Jackson didn't look much like a general. His clothes were usually rumpled, and at times he wore a cap with its visor drawn low. Whether sitting on his favorite horse, Little Sorrel, or on a fence rail in camp, he could usually be found alone. He was also a deeply religious man. He held a religious service almost every day. It was said that his troops were the "prayin'est" in the Confederate army. Jackson strictly observed Sunday as a day of rest, except when he was in battle. He wouldn't even mail a letter if he believed that someone would be carrying it on a Sunday.

Jackson didn't spend much time chitchatting with other officers and certainly not with his soldiers. But all of them respected Jackson as a brilliant and daring general who won battles, even when outnumbered.

Ulysses S. Grant

On the Union side, Ulysses S. Grant was the outstanding general. Looking at his record before the Civil War, however, he might have been voted "least likely to succeed." Like Lee and Jackson, Grant graduated from West Point and fought in the war with Mexico. But there the similarities stopped. Grant was not a top student at West Point. After the Mexican-American War he was assigned to a lonely outpost in the West. He found the daily army duties dull and boring. As a result, he was forced to leave the army. He then tried farming in Missouri but failed. After that he tried selling real estate, but he failed at that, too.

Ulysses S. Grant then returned to his family in Galena, Illinois, where his father gave him a job selling harnesses in the family leather store. That's where he was working when the Civil War began.

Grant promptly volunteered to return to the army and was put in charge of a volunteer regiment. He was thirty-nine years old at the time. In western Tennessee he developed a plan that allowed his troops to capture two Confederate forts. When the commander of one fort asked Grant for his terms of surrender, Grant replied, "no terms except an unconditional and immediate surrender." This firm position brought Grant to the attention of

Lincoln and others in the East. After that, people often said that Grant's initials, U.S., stood for "Unconditional Surrender."

Later, some newspapers and others blamed Grant for being unprepared for the Battle of Shiloh. They demanded that Lincoln

General Grant's war plan was to wear out the Confederate forces.

remove him from command. Lincoln replied, "I can't spare this man. He fights." Lincoln could have added, "And he wins."

Grant once explained his ideas about warfare this way: "The art of war is simple enough. Find out where your enemy is. Get at him as soon as you can. Strike at him as hard as you can, and keep moving on."

Grant's strategy was based on a great advantage he had over the Confederate generals. He knew that with the North's larger population and greater resources, his losses of men and guns could be replaced. He also knew that as the war went on, the other side's losses could not be. So Grant's plan was to force the Confederate armies to fight whenever and wherever he could. Sooner or later he would wear them down. And he did.

Chapter 15
Johnny Reb and Billy Yank

Fighting Men and Boys What of the men, the common soldiers, who did the fighting? What was the Civil War like for them? At the start, it was all glory and adventure. At least that's what volunteers expected when they signed up for service.

The Big Question
···
What was life like for the common soldier during the Civil War?

In the first year, whenever either side called for volunteers, it got all the men that it asked for, and more.

Volunteers rushed to join because they believed in the cause their side was fighting for. And they expected the war to end quickly. Neither side expected the other to fight with real courage. Northerners called Southerners "Rebels," and they nicknamed the Southern soldier "Johnny Reb." Northerners were sure that once Johnny Reb faced Northern troops, he would turn around and run. Southerners had long called Northerners "Yankees," and they nicknamed Northern soldiers "Billy Yank." Southerners were just as sure that Billy Yank would lose his stomach for fighting after one good battle.

Union soldiers

Confederate soldiers

115

Many people who signed up on each side were boys rather than men. The youngest age allowed for a volunteer was eighteen, and there were many of those. Some were younger still—boys of sixteen or seventeen who looked older and didn't want this chance for adventure to pass them by.

Because the South was overwhelmingly rural, nearly all the Southern troops were from farm families. Most had used guns all their life for hunting. The majority of Union soldiers, too, were from farm families. But some Northern troops came from towns and large cities, and few of these city-dwellers had ever held a gun before.

The early enthusiasm for joining the army did not last. Many young men quickly learned that a soldier's life was a hard one.

Conditions in army camps were especially difficult during the winter.

Often it meant marching in the worst kind of weather without enough food and water, all the while carrying fifty pounds of equipment on their backs. "We have been half starved, half frozen, and half drowned," one Union soldier wrote back home. "The mud in Kentucky is awful," a Confederate officer reported. "There is scarcely a private in the army who has a change of clothing of any kind. Hundreds of men are perfectly barefooted." Conditions were so bad that many men fell ill and died before ever seeing battle.

As word of these conditions reached home through letters, the number of volunteers started to drop. To encourage men to enlist, both sides started paying cash **bonuses**—though the Union invested much more money in this approach. In the North, recent Irish and German immigrants saw the bonus money as a way to buy a farm when the war was over, so many of them joined the army. As a result, one in five Union soldiers was an immigrant.

Eventually, though, each side had to turn to the **draft**. That is, they had to require men to serve. This angered people on each side. For one thing, the American government had never drafted men for any previous American war—not the Mexican-American War, not the War of 1812, not even the War for Independence.

> ### Vocabulary
>
> **bonus,** n. extra money that is added to a person's pay
>
> **draft,** n. a system that requires individuals to serve in the military

In addition, the draft laws on both sides seemed unfair to the ordinary citizen. In both the North and the South, a person who was drafted could get out of serving by paying a **substitute** to serve for him. Another way to get out of serving in the Union army was to pay the government $300. For most working people, that was half a year's income—far more money than they could hope to put their hands on. In the South, planters who owned twenty or more slaves could also be excused from service. No wonder so many people on both sides grumbled that this was a rich man's war but a poor man's fight!

> ## Vocabulary
> **substitute,** n. a person or thing that acts in place of another

The Real War

Reading about the battles in a war sometimes makes it seem like the troops were busy fighting all the time. In fact, battles were few and far between, and they usually lasted only a few days. Soldiers spent most days fixing up a camp, repairing equipment, and the like. It was a boring time.

Meals were boring, too. Union troops were supplied with bacon; flour that could only be made into bread; a biscuit called hardtack (which was as hard as it sounds); and coffee to dunk biscuits into. Cattle were often brought along to supply occasional beef. Confederate soldiers received pretty much the same food, except that they got cornmeal instead of wheat flour. Neither army supplied fresh fruits and vegetables, but the soldiers took care of that in their own way. They simply took this food from the farms they marched past.

Even at the start of the war, Billy Yank was better supplied than Johnny Reb. As the war continued, the Confederacy's food

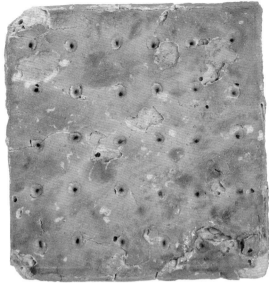

Confederate soldiers often went hungry.   Union soldiers relied on a biscuit called hardtack.

supplies ran low, and the men often went hungry. The South did not make shoes and had to buy them from other countries. As the Northern blockade began to close in, buying goods from other countries became harder and harder to do.

Billy Yank always had a uniform, but Johnny Reb sometimes did not. That doesn't mean Billy Yank was always grateful for his clothes. The Union uniforms were made of wool, which was fine for the winter. But in the hot summer months, the woolen uniform made Billy Yank sweat and itch.

Waiting for battle was boring, but going into battle was terrifying. Every soldier knew that that day or the next might be his last. Many soldiers spent the night before battles praying and writing home to their loved ones. Often, they said in their letters that they did not expect to live through the following days. Sadly, for far too many, their prediction came true.

Those who were wounded on the battlefield were taken to a place almost as dangerous—the army hospital. In fact, most soldiers had already spent time in an army hospital due to sicknesses unrelated to battle. Many never made it out of the hospital alive. Twice as many soldiers died from disease as from battle wounds during the Civil War. They did not have modern drugs. Also, people at that time knew little about germs, but if doctors had simply scrubbed their hands with hot water and soap before moving on to the next patient, many lives would have been saved.

In this "brothers' war," Johnny Reb and Billy Yank often got along pretty well when they were not in battle. It was not unusual for

Doctors in army field hospitals worked under poor conditions.

soldiers doing guard duty for each side to call out to each other. There were taunts, of course, but the men also swapped stories and traded little things. Billy usually wanted Southern tobacco, and Johnny was glad to trade it for more coffee.

African American Soldiers

Soon after Lincoln signed the Emancipation Proclamation, a new group of men joined Billy Yank in the Union army. These men were African Americans. The majority of African American soldiers came from slaveholding states.

Northern African Americans had been volunteering to serve in the army since the war began. However, the army had always turned them down. It had no choice. A law from the 1700s made it illegal for African Americans to serve as soldiers.

The Emancipation Proclamation changed that. In addition to declaring the end of slavery in rebel territory, Lincoln's proclamation also announced that African Americans could serve in the Union army and Union navy.

Frederick Douglass, the great abolitionist, urged African Americans to join the army and help free the 3.5 million slaves. Douglass believed that after African Americans helped fight to save the Union, no one would dare deny them the full rights of citizenship.

Several Northern states formed all-African-American units. The most famous was the Massachusetts 54th Regiment,

Many African Americans were eager to join the Union army and fight to end slavery.

commanded by Colonel Robert Gould Shaw. In the summer of 1863, the 54th Regiment led an attack on Fort Wagner, a Confederate fort on an island in the harbor of Charleston, South Carolina. In spite of heavy cannon fire by Confederate troops, nearly one hundred soldiers forced their way into the fort. There, they fought hand-to-hand against Confederate troops. The bravery of the 54th Regiment in the face of terrible losses won acceptance for African American soldiers everywhere.

Almost one out of every eleven Union soldiers was African American. Altogether, more than 180,000 African Americans served in the Union army. More than 38,000 of those men gave their lives for the Union and the cause of freedom. African Americans served in the Union navy, too. One fifth of all the men who enlisted in the navy were African American—nearly eighteen thousand men. More than 2,800 of them died.

The fighting record of African Americans who served in the Civil War was outstanding. Twenty-one African American soldiers received the Medal of Honor for acts of bravery. This medal is the highest military award in the United States.

Chapter 16
Women and the War Effort

Doing Men's Work During the Civil War, America was still largely a nation of farms. And during the war, women and children on those farms

The Big Question

How did women help the war effort?

still had all their regular tasks to perform. They also had to do much more. With the men off fighting, women and children had to do the men's work as well.

In the South, many women had to take charge of managing the large farms and plantations. On the plantations, there were still slaves to do the physical work. However, most Southerners with small farms didn't own slaves. In these families, the women had to do all the work their husbands had done before.

The same was true of farm women in the North and West. A traveler to western farm states in 1863 reported that "women were in the fields everywhere, driving the reapers . . . and loading grain." As one woman explained: "Harvesting isn't any harder than cooking, washing, and ironing over a red-hot stove in July and August—only we have to do both now. My three brothers went into the army, all my

During the Civil War, women had to take over many jobs that were previously done by men.

—[SEE PAGE 570.]

cousins, most of the young men about here, and the men we used to hire. So there's no help to be got but women, and the crops must be got in all the same, you know."

Even without men doing their normal tasks, the farms in the North and West produced as much food as they had before the war. As a result, thanks to the hard work of women, Union troops never went hungry during the war, and workers in the cities also had plenty to eat.

In addition, women on both sides made bandages, knitted socks, and sewed clothing to send to the soldiers. They also kept up the spirits of their men with letters from home.

Women served on both sides in other ways, too. Some carried mail for the armies. Many sewed uniforms or worked in weapons factories. Others worked as **spies**. One of the North's spies was Harriet Tubman, the famed conductor on the Underground Railroad. On the battlefield, there were several hundred women who disguised themselves as men so they could fight.

There were various other organizations whose members did heroic service. One of them was the Army Corps of Nurses. About three thousand women served as nurses during the war. Compared to the more than three million men serving in the two armies,

Harriet Tubman served as a spy for the Union during the Civil War.

that doesn't sound like a lot. But in those days, nursing was a man's job. Before the war, a woman couldn't be hired as a nurse. Once the war came, however, so many nurses were needed that women were finally accepted into the profession.

On the Confederate side, Sally Tompkins ran a private hospital in Richmond, Virginia. In this hospital she cared for both Confederate soldiers and Union prisoners. To Tompkins, a life was a life, and it didn't matter whether the person wore Confederate gray or Union blue. She and her nurses saved hundreds of lives.

Clara Barton

One of the truly heroic nurses on the Union side was Clara Barton. Even before the war, Clara Barton always seemed to be breaking new ground. As a schoolteacher in New Jersey, she opened the first free school in that state. Before that, parents had to pay to send their children to school. Later, she became the first woman to hold a regular job in the federal government when she worked as a clerk in the U.S. Patent Office in Washington, D.C.

Barton always found her greatest happiness in helping others. When the Civil War broke out, she threw herself into the Union cause by helping its soldiers. Living in Washington, she provided food and comfort to the homesick soldiers who poured into the city during the early months of the war. At first, Barton collected supplies herself. She wrote letters home for those who couldn't write. As news of her work spread, churches and citizens' groups sent bandages and other supplies. Soon her apartment was overflowing with boxes, and she had to rent a **warehouse** to store them all.

Barton was not satisfied with staying in Washington while men went into battle. She asked army officials to allow her to help the men at the **battlefront**. As she wrote later in the war, "My business is [stopping the flow] of blood and feeding men; my post [is] the open field between the bullet and the hospital." The officials turned down her request at first, but she persisted until they finally said yes.

She first appeared on the battlefront in August 1862. The field hospital was almost out of dressings for wounds when Barton arrived with her mule-drawn wagon filled with supplies. An army **surgeon** wrote, "I thought that night if heaven ever sent out a holy angel, she must be the one, her assistance was so timely." Barton helped the surgeon bandage the wounded.

After that, Clara Barton was on the scene of many battles with her wagonloads of bandages, coffee, jellies, brandy, crackers, and cans of soup and beef.

The Civil War brought women like Clara Barton to the battlefields to serve as nurses.

At the Battle of Antietam, she was the only woman allowed at the front. She followed the cannons up to the front lines. For a long time her wagon provided the only medical supplies available.

On the battlefields, Clara Barton often worked for days with almost no sleep. She cared for the wounded in the field, and in tents, houses, churches—wherever shelter could be found. She fed them. She wrote letters home for them. She comforted the wounded and the dying.

Upon her return to Washington, Barton was called to serve at Lincoln Hospital. As she entered one ward, seventy men—each of whom had received her care—rose to salute her. She earned the nickname that soldiers gave her: "Angel of the Battlefield." Later, after the war ended, Clara Barton founded the American Red Cross.

Soldiers called Clara Barton "Angel of the Battlefield."

Chapter 17
The Tide Turns

A New Year As the year 1863 began, things continued to go badly for the Union on the battlefields of the East. Just the month before, in December 1862, the Union army tried once again to take Richmond. But before they could get there, Robert E. Lee defeated them in a brilliant victory at Fredericksburg.

> ### The Big Question
>
> Why was the Battle of Gettysburg important and still remembered today?

In May 1863, a Union army of 130,000 men headed toward Richmond again. Lee's army, with only half as many troops, took them on at Chancellorsville, Virginia. Once again, Lee and Stonewall Jackson managed to come out on top through their daring strategy.

The South did suffer a great loss at Chancellorsville, however. In the confusion of battle, Jackson was mistakenly shot by one of his own men. He lost his left arm. For a time, it seemed he might recover, but then infection set in, and Jackson died.

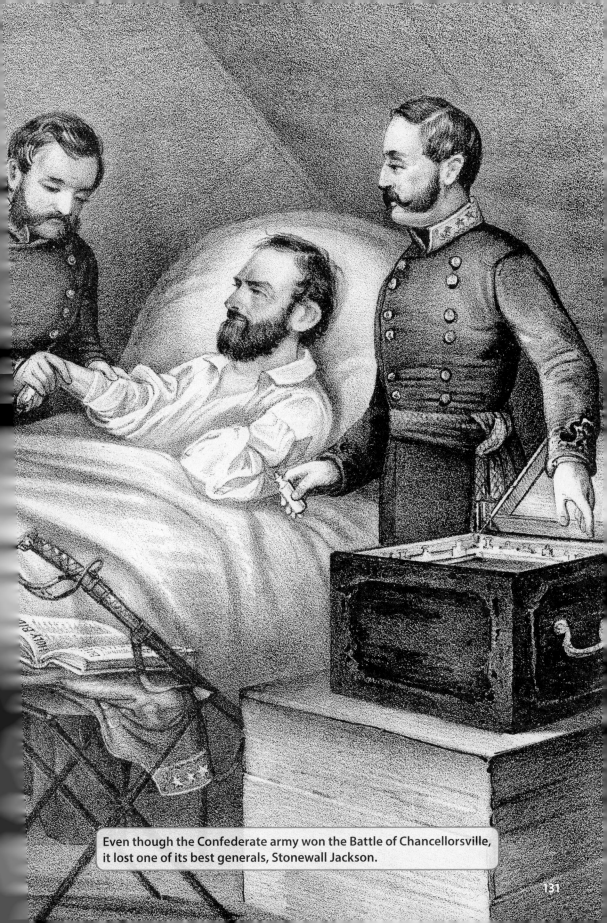

Even though the Confederate army won the Battle of Chancellorsville, it lost one of its best generals, Stonewall Jackson.

Chancellorsville was Robert E. Lee's most brilliant victory. No one knew it then, but it was his last important victory.

In the West, General Grant's army continued to gain victories in western Tennessee and Mississippi. By spring of 1863, there were only two rebel **strongholds** remaining along the Mississippi. The most important of these was Vicksburg, Mississippi. If Vicksburg fell to the Union army, the Union would control the entire Mississippi River. The western states of the Confederacy would be cut off from the others, and the anaconda would squeeze ever more tightly around the Confederacy.

It looked like that would happen. Just two weeks after Lee's victory at Chancellorsville, Lee learned that Grant had laid **siege** to Vicksburg. That means he had surrounded it and could prevent supplies and troops from helping the thirty thousand Confederate troops who were trapped there. It seemed only a matter of time until the city fell to Unconditional Surrender Grant.

The siege of Vicksburg made Lee see that he needed to do more than fight a defensive war against invading Union troops. He needed to go on the attack. He needed to take the war into the North and win battles on Northern soil. Then the enemy might finally lose heart and agree to peace.

General Grant laid siege to the Confederate stronghold of Vicksburg.

Lee's plan was to march across Maryland and into southern Pennsylvania. A victory there would threaten both Washington, D.C., and Philadelphia. Pennsylvania was far from his home base in Virginia, but Lee knew his army could live off the food grown on Maryland's and Pennsylvania's rich farmlands. He would be able to seize other supplies, like desperately needed shoes, as he captured towns.

Gettysburg

Robert E. Lee and his Army of Northern Virginia arrived in the town of Gettysburg, Pennsylvania, on July 1, 1863. As it happened, a Union army led by General George Meade was also in the area.

Lincoln placed Meade in charge of the Union armies in the East only three days before.

No one had planned for a battle to take place in Gettysburg, but there they were, face to face. For the next three days—July 1, 2, and 3—a battle raged between the Confederate and Union armies. Again and again, Lee's forces attacked. Again and again, Union forces threw them back.

On July 3, Lee decided on one final attack, which he hoped would break the Union's resistance. At about two o'clock in the afternoon, 12,500 men under the command of General George Pickett emerged from the woods and began their advance across an open field toward the Union's line. The attack, later called Pickett's Charge, was incredibly brave, but it failed. The Union army opened fire with its big guns and with its muskets. Pickett's army, as one Confederate officer reported, "just seemed to melt away in the blue . . . smoke which now covered the hill. Nothing but stragglers came back."

With a third of his army lost, there was nothing for Lee to do but retreat. On July 4, his exhausted, downhearted men started back toward Virginia in a pouring rain. To get there, they would have to cross the Potomac River. President Lincoln, informed of the battle's events, realized that this was a chance to trap Lee and the rest of his army. He **telegraphed** General Meade, urging him to pursue Lee. But Meade, like McClellan before him, was

> **Vocabulary**
>
> **telegraph,** v. to communicate over long distances by sending signals through wires

The Battle of Gettysburg resulted in the highest number of casualties during the entire Civil War.

too cautious. By the time Meade was ready to move, Lee's army had safely crossed the Potomac River and was out of the Union's reach. "We had them within our grasp," complained the frustrated president. But once more, Lee had escaped.

Even so, Gettysburg was a major defeat for the Confederacy. Never again would its army invade the North. The tide of battle in the East now turned in the Union's favor. Meanwhile, in the West, Vicksburg surrendered to Grant on that same July 4, giving the Union control of the entire Mississippi River. Independence Day 1863 turned out to be a great day for the Union.

Some months later, the citizens of Gettysburg held a ceremony to honor those who had died in the great battle. To give the main speech, they had invited Edward Everett of Massachusetts, known as the greatest public speaker of that time. President Lincoln was invited to make a few remarks. But he and everyone else understood that it was Everett who was to be the star of the occasion.

And Everett did, indeed, give a speech that lasted nearly two hours. Near the end of the afternoon, President Lincoln was called upon for his remarks. He spoke for just two minutes.

It's funny how things work out sometimes. Edward Everett spoke for two hours, and while he gave a fine speech, no one today remembers a word of it. Abraham Lincoln spoke for just two minutes, and his speech has become one of the most famous in American history. Lincoln wanted to use this speech to explain the real meaning of the war. The war was really about the ideas found in the Declaration of Independence. It was about liberty, and about equal rights, and about democracy. Most of the president's listeners that day didn't quite realize the importance of what he said, but Everett knew it immediately. Walking over to Lincoln, Everett said, "Mr. President, I should be glad if I could flatter myself that I came as near to the central idea of this occasion in two hours, as you did in two minutes."

Fourscore and seven years ago our fathers brought forth on this continent a new nation, conceived in liberty and dedicated to the proposition that all men are created equal.

Now we are engaged in a great civil war, testing whether that nation or any nation so conceived and so dedicated can long endure. We are met on a great battlefield of that war. We have come to dedicate a portion of that field as a final resting-place for those who here gave their lives that that nation might live. It is altogether fitting and proper that we should do this.

But in a larger sense, we cannot dedicate, we cannot **consecrate**, we cannot **hallow** this ground. The brave men, living and dead who struggled here have consecrated it far above our poor power to add or detract. The world will little note nor long remember what we say here, but it can never forget what they did here. It is for us the living rather to be dedicated here to the unfinished work which they who fought here have thus far so nobly advanced. It is rather for us to be here dedicated to the great task remaining before us—that from these honored dead we take increased devotion to that cause for which they gave the last full measure of devotion—that we here highly resolve that these dead shall not have died in vain, that this nation under God shall have a new birth of freedom, and that government of the people, by the people, for the people shall not perish from the earth.

—The Gettysburg Address by Abraham Lincoln, November 19, 1863

> **Vocabulary**
>
> **consecrate,** v. to declare something sacred or holy
>
> **hallow,** v. to honor or respect

Chapter 18
Confederate Problems Mount

States' Rights By the end of 1863, the Confederate States of America had problems not only on the battlefield but back home as well. A lot of these problems had to do with the kind of government the Confederacy had set up.

The Big Question

What problems did the Confederacy have at home?

Southern states said that under the Constitution, states had certain rights that the federal government could not interfere with. If the federal government interfered with slavery in a state, for example, or if it passed a law that the people of a state didn't want, like a tax law, then the state had the right to drop out of the Union. This idea came to be called **states' rights**.

> **Vocabulary**
>
> **states' rights,** n. political powers that belong to state governments under the Constitution; also, the belief that the federal government should have less power and state governments should have more power

IN GOD WE TRUST

A Confederate soldier holds the stars and bars, the first national flag of the Confederacy.

Naturally, when the seceding states wrote a constitution for the Confederacy, they made sure the idea of states' rights was in it. And you can be sure that any time leaders of the Southern states didn't want to do something, they cried, "Our states' rights are being violated!"

So when the Confederate Congress voted for new taxes to pay for the war, a lot of Southern **governors** dragged their feet in collecting them. "States' rights!" they shouted. North Carolina had plenty of

uniforms and blankets, but it kept them for soldiers from its own state and refused to share with other Confederate troops. "We don't have to contribute them to the Confederacy. States' rights," said the state's leaders. Georgia had ten thousand men in a state army but refused to let Confederate commanders give them orders. "States' rights." And South Carolina—the first state to secede from the Union—at one point actually threatened to secede from the Confederacy! A war cannot be run that way.

King Cotton

The confederacy also made a very bad prediction. Great Britain had the world's largest textile, or cloth, industry. France was not far behind. Both got most of their raw cotton from the South. Would Britain and France allow the Northern blockade to cut off their supply of cotton, forcing their factories to close and throwing their people out of work?

"Not a chance," said the South. Even before secession, that's what a confident senator from South Carolina told his fellow senators from the North. "What would happen if no cotton were furnished for three years? England would topple headlong and carry the whole civilized world with her, (except) the South." That's why, this senator warned the North, "you dare not make war on cotton. No power on earth dare make war upon it. Cotton is King!"

It turned out that Southern leaders were wrong. For one thing, when the Civil War began, Great Britain had plenty of cotton in its warehouses—much more than it needed right then. So it didn't have to buy a lot of cotton from the South right away to keep its factories going and its workers working. Also, Great Britain knew that challenging the Union's blockade might lead to war

The cotton industry in the South could not survive without African American slaves.

with the United States, and it didn't want that. Finally, British working people were against slavery and didn't want their government to support the last great slaveholding power in the world. Especially after the Emancipation Proclamation, they sided with the North.

So, the South never got the help it expected from Great Britain. It wasn't able to sell its cotton, and it wasn't able to buy the **manufactured goods** and other supplies it needed so badly. As time went on, that hurt the Confederacy's chances more and more.

Jefferson Davis

Government leadership was another problem for the Confederacy. No one could blame Jefferson Davis, its president, for not being another Lincoln. Who could be? But Davis lacked certain skills that would have made him a better leader.

Oddly, Jefferson Davis and Abraham Lincoln were born less than one hundred miles from each other in Kentucky and only eight months apart. Like the Lincoln family, the Davis family was poor. A few years after Jefferson was born, the family moved to the Mississippi Territory. Jefferson's father proved to be better at choosing farmland than Abraham's, and the Davis family grew cotton and soon became rich.

Jefferson Davis went to the military school at West Point, and although he was not much of a student, he graduated and served in the U.S. Army for a number of years. When his family gave him a large piece of land along the Mississippi River, he left the army to raise cotton.

Like every big planter, Davis owned slaves. He was one of the kinder slaveholders in Mississippi. He rarely punished his slaves, and he allowed them to learn to read and write—something few owners did. But he was as firm in his belief as many other Southerners that slavery was a good thing for both African Americans and white people, and that it must be preserved.

As he grew older, Jefferson Davis read books on history, politics, literature, poetry, and military strategy. By the time he entered Congress in 1845, he was one of the best-educated men in government.

Jefferson Davis left Congress to fight in the Mexican-American War. He later served as a U.S. senator and as a secretary of war. When the Southern states formed the Confederate States of America, they chose Jefferson Davis to be president. It was a job Davis did not want, but he agreed to serve. His wife said that when he told her he had been chosen, he spoke "as a man might speak of a sentence of death."

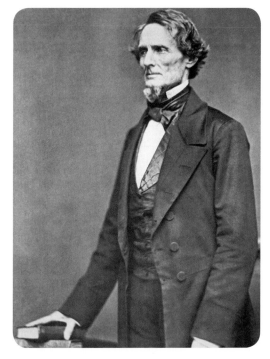

Jefferson Davis served in the U.S. government for many years but chose the Confederacy when the Southern states seceded.

Jefferson Davis sits with the first Confederate cabinet.

The job was very difficult. The new government was starting from scratch. It had no offices, no employees, and no postal service. President Davis's first office—his "White House"—was in a hotel

parlor, a room usually set aside for entertaining guests. Davis worked very hard, but he allowed himself to get bogged down in small details that took a lot of his time.

Davis was also too sure of himself when it came to military strategy. He often overruled generals who were better at running a war than he was. He interfered so much with the War Department that five different secretaries of war quit.

On the whole, Davis did not deal well with people. He was difficult and stubborn. Rather than try to win over those who disagreed with him, he quarreled and made enemies.

By the start of 1864, the Confederate army was struggling. With the fall of Vicksburg, the West was lost, and so were most of Kentucky and Tennessee. In the East, Union armies were once again carrying the fight onto Southern soil. But a Union victory was still not a certainty. Even President Lincoln felt unsure that the Union would be victorious.

Fortunately for the president he had finally found the general he had been looking for, the one who would fight and fight and fight some more, and never stop pursuing the enemy. That general was, of course, Ulysses S. Grant who, in the spring of 1864, took charge of all the Union armies.

Chapter 19
The War Draws to a Close

A Battle in the Wilderness Fight and fight some more. Then chase. That is exactly what Grant and his army did in the spring of 1864. Once again, the scene was northern Virginia. Once again, the prize was Richmond. And once again, the armies met and did battle near Chancellorsville, where one year earlier Lee had won his most brilliant victory.

The Big Question

How did the Union finally defeat the Confederacy?

But this time it was different.

The fighting took place in a dense forest known as the Wilderness. Grant's army outnumbered Lee's by nearly two to one. The Battle of the Wilderness raged for two days. It was a terrible, bloody battle, and at the end, Grant had lost more men than Lee. But Grant knew that his losses could be replaced and Lee's could not.

Lee had to pull back, stopping several times to fight some more. Grant's army continued to press forward toward Richmond and Petersburg, an important railroad center near Richmond. Finally, Grant had his armies in position to begin a siege in front of the two cities. That summer,

Grant's victory at the Battle of the Wilderness came with a high loss of life.

autumn, and winter, Grant's army kept Lee's troops in Richmond and Petersburg from breaking out. They could only retreat and abandon the cities.

Meanwhile, General William Tecumseh Sherman, who was now in charge of Union forces in the West, prepared to tighten the squeeze of the anaconda. With an army of ninety thousand, Sherman set out from Tennessee toward the important railroad city of Atlanta. Sherman didn't worry about food for his army. He would take that from the farms along the way.

In September 1864, Atlanta fell to Union troops. From there, Sherman led his army on a "march to the sea." During the march he used a method of warfare sometimes called "total war." Sherman not only fought the other side's soldiers, but he also destroyed farms, burned warehouses and barns, wrecked shops,

The Union army captured Atlanta in September, 1864.

and tore up rail lines. Although civilians were not targeted, Sherman did whatever he could to weaken the enemy.

In December, the coastal city of Savannah, Georgia, fell. By January, Sherman was in South Carolina. By March, he was in North Carolina. Everywhere his armies went, they left behind destruction, and hatred and bitterness, too.

By this time, Abraham Lincoln had been reelected to a second term in office. The presidential election during the war showed the strength of American democracy, that even during a civil war the laws of the Constitution were followed. Lincoln's opponent was none other than the general he had removed from command, George B. McClellan. McClellan said that if elected, he would end the war quickly. To people who were tired of the war, sick of the terrible losses, and even fearful of actually losing, that was very appealing.

Lincoln, determined to see the war through to the end in order to preserve the Union and free the slaves, could make no such promise. For a time, he expected to lose the election. Then came the news of Sherman's capture of Atlanta and of several other Union victories. Northern spirits rose, and Lincoln easily won reelection.

By the time Lincoln's second term began in March 1865, it was clear that the Confederacy was doomed. Lincoln realized that it was time to get Americans to focus on the next great task before them: reuniting the nation. Would it be possible, after four years of killing and destruction, for people to understand the pain and suffering of those on the other side? Many Northerners talked of revenge. They wanted to get even for what the South's secession had caused. Many wanted to treat the Southerners as a conquered people.

"With Malice Toward None"

That was not Lincoln's way. The Union was preserved; slavery was ended. For Lincoln, that was enough. The job now was to get back to being one nation, the United States of America, and to fulfill that nation's promise of greatness. President Lincoln announced his plan for restoring the Union. It was a plan to bring the Southern states back into the Union quickly and without harsh punishment. In his second inaugural address, on March 4, 1865, he urged Americans to adopt a forgiving spirit as they set about this task:

With **malice** toward none; with charity for all; with firmness in the right, as God gives us to see the right, let us strive on to finish the work we are in; to **bind** up the nation's wounds; to care for him who shall have borne the battle, and for his widow, and his orphan—to do all which may achieve and cherish a just, and lasting peace among ourselves, and with all nations.

> **Vocabulary**
>
> **malice,** n. a desire to hurt another person
>
> **bind,** v. to tie up

All that remained was for Grant's armies to finish the job. A month after Lincoln's speech, Petersburg and Richmond fell. Lee tried to gather his weary and hungry army once more, but Union forces followed him. There was, finally, no way out. On April 9, Lee sent an officer with a white flag of surrender to the Union army and asked to meet with General Grant.

The surrender took place at a house in the village of Appomattox Court House, Virginia. Grant wrote out the terms of surrender and treated the defeated enemy with great respect. The Confederates would turn in their weapons, except for the officers' small guns. All were free to leave. And, added Grant, "let all the men who claim to own a horse or mule take the animals home with them to work their little farms." It was a generous offer, and Lee thanked Grant for it. The two generals saluted each other. Then Lee climbed on his horse, Traveller, looked thoughtfully over the field of Union soldiers, and rode away.

The American Civil War was over.

General Lee surrendered on April 9, 1865, at Appomattox Court House, Virginia.

Chapter 20
The Death of President Lincoln

Victory at Last! News of Lee's surrender at Appomattox Court House on April 9 quickly reached Washington, D.C. The next day, cannons boomed, fireworks exploded over the Potomac River, and the Stars and Stripes hung everywhere. The celebration spilled over to April 11. That afternoon a crowd gathered at the White House called out, "Speech! Speech!"

The Big Question

Why did John Wilkes Booth kill President Lincoln?

John Wilkes Booth

In the crowd outside the White House was an actor named John Wilkes Booth. When President Lincoln finished speaking, Booth turned to a friend and snarled, "That's the last speech he will ever make."

Lincoln had often seen Booth perform at Ford's Theatre, which was not far from the White House. Lincoln had enjoyed the actor's work. He did not know, however, that Booth was his mortal enemy.

John Wilkes Booth

Even as a teenager, John Wilkes Booth had talked about doing great deeds someday. "I must have fame! Fame!" he told friends. He said he had to do "something never before accomplished; something no other man would probably ever do."

Booth was a **racist** through and through. He believed that slavery was good and that the South's cause was just. During the war he had served as a **secret agent** for the Confederacy. In his mind, no one was more responsible for the defeat of his beloved South than President Lincoln. And for that, Lincoln had to pay.

Booth's first plan was to kidnap Lincoln, take him to Richmond, and offer to exchange him for all the Confederate soldiers who were prisoners of war. When that didn't work, he decided to kill Lincoln.

President Lincoln had received many threatening letters during his presidency, but he simply threw them away. He refused to take such threats seriously. After all, no one had ever killed an American president before. When friends urged him to use guards, Lincoln said that having guards protect him against angry Southerners "would only put the idea [of killing him] into their heads." And "as to the crazy folks, why I must only take my chances."

Lincoln Shot at Ford's Theatre

On Friday, April 14—three days after Lincoln's speech—the president met with his cabinet and a special guest, General Grant.

Grant and his wife were invited by the Lincolns to attend a play with them that evening at Ford's Theatre. Grant had to decline the invitation, and Lincoln really didn't feel like going without him. But he knew that his wife, Mary, looked forward to going, and the people of Washington were expecting him to make an appearance. So the Lincolns went to the theater – and so did John Wilkes Booth!

Sitting in the special presidential box just to the side of the stage, the president seemed to enjoy the show. Booth, who was in the audience, picked his time well. He knew the play on stage, every line of it. In the third act there was one line that always brought a lot of laughter. That moment—with the laughter distracting the audience—would be his moment to strike.

After shooting President Lincoln, John Wilkes Booth jumped from the presidential box onto the stage.

Booth approached the door at the back of the presidential box. The guard who was supposed to be there had left his post. Booth entered. As the actor on stage said his line and the audience laughed, Booth raised his pistol and, from six feet away, fired into the back of the president's head.

Booth then moved quickly to the railing of the box and shouted, "Revenge for the South." He jumped down onto the stage and shouted, "*Sic semper tyrannis*," a Latin phrase that means, "Thus always to tyrants."

Booth broke his leg when he landed on the stage but he still managed to escape. As a well-known actor, he was easily recognized. Booth avoided capture for nearly two weeks, but he was finally found hiding in a barn and was shot.

As for the wounded president, he was carried

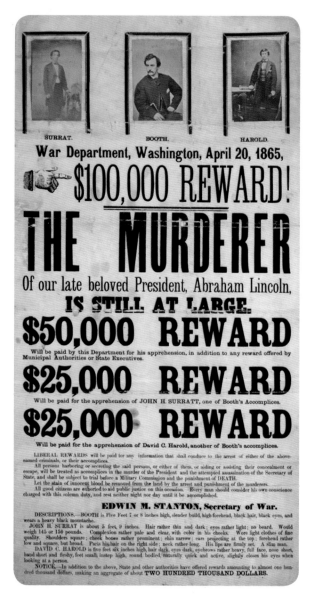

Booth escaped the theater and hid for two weeks before being found.

to a house across the street, where friends and a doctor tried to make him comfortable. But there was no hope that he would live. Even the most modern of medical care today could not have saved him. The following morning he breathed his last. "Now," said his secretary of war, Edwin Stanton, "he belongs to the ages."

Booth believed he was striking a blow for the South. He could not have been more mistaken. It was Lincoln who had said, "With malice toward none; with charity for all." It was Lincoln who held out the best hope for a peace without bitterness and revenge. It was Lincoln who spoke of bringing the Southern states back into the Union as quickly as possible.

And now Lincoln was gone.

Chapter 21
The South in Ruins

A Broad Streak of Ruin At the end of the Civil War, the South was a devastated land. Travelers to the region were shocked by what they saw. Wherever General Sherman's army had marched in Georgia and South Carolina, wrote one traveler, the countryside "looked for many miles like a broad black streak of ruin."

The Big Question

What was life like in the South after the Civil War?

In other words, so much had been burned. In Tennessee, one visitor stated, "The trail of war is visible . . . in burnt-up (cotton) gin houses, ruined bridges, mills, and factories." And in Virginia, wrote yet another, "The barns are all burned, chimneys standing without houses and houses standing without roofs, or doors or windows."

Fields that once produced fine harvests of cotton, tobacco, and grain were covered with weeds. Small farms were destroyed. Nearly half the South's farm animals were gone. Railroad tracks were torn up. Whatever factories the South had before the war were now mostly destroyed. Many Southerners, both white and African American, were without food, clothing, or any way to make a living.

Many cities in the South, including Charleston, South Carolina, were left in ruins.

The human losses were even worse. Close to one-third of the men and boys who put on the gray uniform of the Confederacy had died during the war. Even more were wounded, some so badly they would never be the same again. In 1866, the year after the war ended, the state of Mississippi spent one out of every five tax dollars it collected to buy artificial arms and legs for its veterans.

As for the former slaves, the war brought them freedom. In the first months after the war, a good many African Americans left their old plantations just so they could experience their newfound freedom. They wanted to know what it was like to go wherever they wanted without having to get permission from an owner. One former slave told her former owner that she just could not stay and continue to cook for her. "If I stay here," she said, "I'll never know I am free."

Many freed slaves had an even more important reason for taking to the road. They hoped to find family members who had been sold and separated from them.

But most of the former slaves stayed right where they were. This may seem surprising, but they had to make a living. The best chance of doing that was to get hired to work on the land of their former

Many freed slaves left their old plantations to find family members and to start new lives.

owners, or to rent some of the land to farm for themselves. Even though they were now free and could keep the fruits of their labor, their lives didn't improve much.

Even while the war was going on, Congress realized it would have to help people get back on their feet. Just a month before the war's end, Congress created the Freedmen's Bureau. Freedmen were the former slaves. The Freedmen's Bureau provided food, clothing, fuel, and medical supplies to needy Southern whites as well as former slaves.

The Freedmen's Bureau had its greatest success in education. It set up more than four thousand schools where former slaves could learn to read and write. Northern churches sent thousands of dedicated women and men to teach in these schools. Before the Civil War, slaves were usually forbidden to learn those skills. Now African American Southerners flocked to these schools—not just children but adults, too. Many of the adults were deeply religious people who had long wanted to read the Bible for themselves.

One thing the Freedmen's Bureau did not do, however, was give the former slaves their own land. That was a shame, because with their own land, African Americans would have had a chance to support themselves and become truly independent. As one former slave said, "All I want is to get to own four or five **acres** of land, that I can build me a little house on and call my home." Another said, "Give us our own land and we will take care of ourselves. But without land, the old masters can hire us or starve us, as they please."

> **Vocabulary**
>
> **acre,** n. an area of land that measures 4,840 square yards

This Freedmen's Bureau school was opened in Richmond, Virginia, after the Civil War.

For a time, African Americans were excited by a rumor that the government would give them forty acres and a mule to get their new lives started. However, it was only a rumor. The only way to give land to the former slaves was to take it away from someone else, such as the former slave owners. A few people in Congress were willing to do that, but most were not, so it did not happen.

Sharecropping

Many of the freed slaves continued to farm the lands of their former masters. However, a big problem had to be worked out first. When the Confederacy collapsed, all of its money immediately became worthless. Southern banks also went out of business. Few Southerners had U.S. money. Owners of the land had no money to pay wages to their workers, and the freedmen who wanted to rent land had no money to pay for it. The problem was solved by developing a system called sharecropping.

Sharecropping worked this way: The owners let the freedmen use some of their land, gave them seed, and lent them plows, tools, and mules to work with. In return, the freedmen gave the owners a share of the crops they raised. Usually they split the crops half and half.

The sharecropping system was used all through the South. Nine out of ten former slave families became sharecroppers, and many poor white families did, too.

Many freed African Americans became sharecroppers on the land they had farmed as slaves.

Chapter 22
The Struggle over Reconstruction

Uniting the States For all its terrible cost in lives and money, the Civil War settled one thing for sure. No state, or any number of states, can secede from the Union. The union of states is permanent. However, a number of other important questions remained.

The Big Question

How did Andrew Johnson's ideas of reconstruction differ from the Radical Republicans'?

What should be done with the states that had tried to leave the Union? Should they have to do anything to get back their full rights as states? If so, what? Should it be easy for them to return to normal statehood, or should they be punished? Who had the right to decide these questions, the president or Congress?

For President Lincoln the answers were simple. The reason for fighting the war in the first place was to preserve the Union. He argued that the South was in a state of rebellion and that it had not left the Union. Therefore, the two sections of the Union should be **reconciled** as

Vocabulary

reconcile, v. to return to a friendly relationship after a conflict

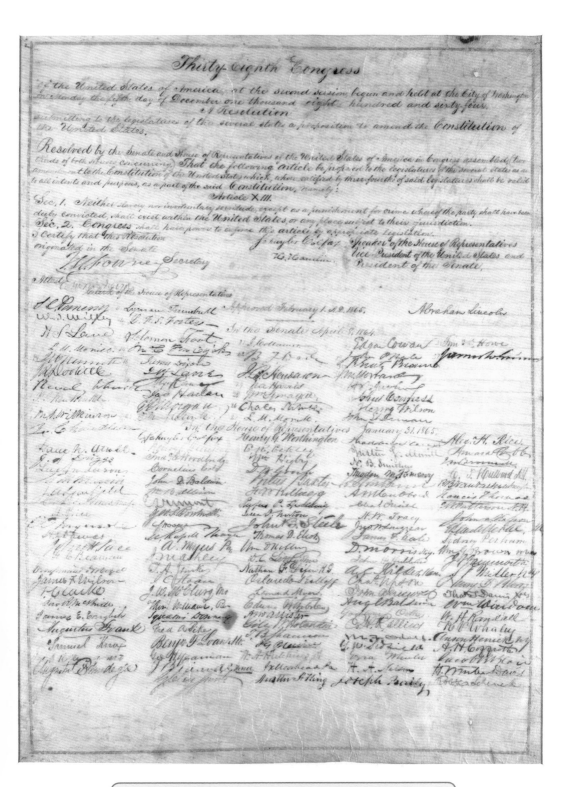

This is a congressional copy of the Thirteenth Amendment.

quickly as possible. Still, there were certain things the Southern states should have to do. One was that each state must **ratify**,

or approve, the Thirteenth Amendment to the U.S. Constitution. The Thirteenth Amendment outlaws slavery. Once a state had done those things, it could write a new state constitution, elect a state government, and send representatives to Congress. Lincoln had meant what he said: "With malice toward none; with charity for all." He wanted to "bind up the nation's wounds" as quickly as possible.

President Andrew Johnson

But now Lincoln was dead, and Andrew Johnson was president. Would Johnson share Lincoln's views? People looked to Johnson's background for clues as to where he might stand.

Johnson had grown up poor in North Carolina and later made his living as a tailor in Greenville, Tennessee. Although he had never been to school, he taught himself the basics of reading and writing, and with the help of his wife, he became quite good at both.

His neighbors elected him to the Tennessee legislature, and he later served as governor, congressman, and senator from that state. Although Johnson had owned several slaves, he strongly disliked the wealthy slave-owning planters of the South and had a strong sympathy for the common people.

Most important, Andrew Johnson was a strong believer in the Union. When Tennessee joined the Confederacy, Johnson refused to follow his state and remained in the U.S. Senate. He was the

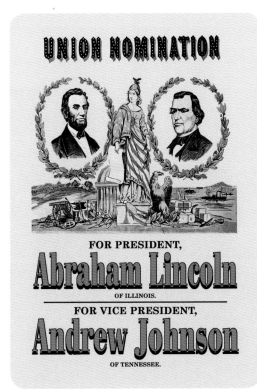

Andrew Johnson was the first vice president to reach the presidency following the assassination of the president.

only Southern senator from a Confederate state to do so. When President Lincoln ran for reelection in 1864, he chose Johnson to run for the vice presidency with him, even though Lincoln was a Republican and Johnson was a Democrat.

At first, some of the congressmen who opposed Lincoln's plan for restoring the Union thought that Johnson would side with them. "Johnson, we have faith in you," said one of those congressmen, "there'll be no trouble now."

However, these congressmen had guessed wrong. Johnson opposed slavery, but that was as far as it went. He believed that the Union should be restored quickly, and except for getting rid of slavery, he didn't think the South should be forced to make other major changes.

Johnson soon announced that he would follow Lincoln's plan, with a few changes. This plan to restore the Union quickly became known as Presidential **Reconstruction**. To reconstruct is to rebuild, or to restore. By the end of 1865, most of the Southern states had done what they were required to do and were ready to be restored to the Union. That took care of the matter, as far as President Johnson was concerned.

Congress and Radical Reconstruction

Congress, however, disagreed with President Johnson. They were not happy with Presidential Reconstruction. To begin with, Congress demanded, who ever said it was up to the president to decide on Reconstruction? That should be the right of Congress, not of the president. There would be no reconstruction of the Union until *Congress* said so.

Furthermore, Congress wanted Reconstruction to be much harder on the South than the president did. After all, wasn't it the South that wanted to break up the Union in the first place? Who started the Civil War? Who was responsible for the loss of life—260,000–300,000 Confederate soldiers and 360,000 Union soldiers? After all the pain the war caused, members of Congress believed the Southern states should not be allowed back into the Union so easily.

Some members of Congress pointed out that the Southern states had shown no sign of regret about the war. Instead, the

South was defiant and that was reflected in the men they had chosen to represent them in Congress. Four were Confederate generals, eight were colonels, and six had served in Jefferson Davis's Confederate cabinet. Georgia was even sending Alexander Stephens, the vice president of the Confederacy, to the U.S. Senate! Why, these were some of the very people who had led the rebellion. And now they expected to be welcomed into Congress and to share in making laws for the country!

Congress believed that while Southern states had given up slavery, they had not changed their attitudes toward African Americans. Every one of the Southern states had passed laws,

After the war, Southern states passed laws that limited the rights and freedoms of African Americans.

known as **Black Codes**, to limit the new freedom of African Americans. One Southern state, for example, allowed African Americans to work only on farms or as housekeepers. Another state said that African Americans could not change jobs or travel from place to place. In another state, they weren't allowed to own land in a city.

If these states were allowed to return to the Union under the Presidential Reconstruction plan, Congress was concerned there would be no way to protect the rights of African Americans in the South.

Congress demanded a more **radical** plan for Reconstruction. Radical often means extreme, but here it meant "getting to the root of the problem" by changing the laws of the South and the nation. Supporters of this view were known as Radical Republicans.

In December 1865, Congress blocked Presidential Reconstruction, and for the next year, President Johnson and those in favor of Radical Reconstruction argued angrily over what to do about the South. In the spring of that year, Congress passed the Civil Rights Act of 1866. The purpose of this act was to protect the rights of the former slaves against the Black Codes. President Johnson **vetoed** it, but Congress passed it over the president's veto. The Civil Rights Act became law.

The Radical Republicans then proposed one of the most important of all amendments

> ## Vocabulary
>
> **"Black Codes,"** (phrase) laws passed in Southern states to limit the freedoms of African Americans after the Civil War
>
> **radical,** adj. favoring large or widespread changes
>
> **veto,** v. to reject or refuse to approve a law

to the Constitution: the Fourteenth Amendment. This is a long and complicated amendment, but it has a few main points:

- The amendment made all former slaves citizens of the United States. This overturned the Supreme Court's ruling in the *Dred Scott* decision that African Americans could not be citizens.

- The amendment prevents states from making any law that limits the rights of African Americans.

- The amendment prohibits states from taking away a person's life, liberty, or property unfairly.

- Finally, it requires states to treat all people equally under the law.

Radical Republicans said that the Fourteenth Amendment would finally protect the former slaves. They said that ratifying it should be the price each Southern state must pay to reenter the Union. When one Southern state, Tennessee, did ratify the amendment, it was promptly readmitted to the Union.

President Johnson, though, was opposed to this amendment. He quietly told the other Southern states that once he won the struggle with Congress, they wouldn't have to ratify it. Those states took Johnson's advice and refused to ratify the amendment. It was a big mistake.

When elections were held for Congress in 1866, many more Radical Republican candidates were voted into office. That finished Presidential Reconstruction. From then on, the Radical Republicans made it clear that they would be in charge of Reconstruction.

Chapter 23
Congressional Reconstruction

Who were these Radical Republicans? What did they believe? What did it mean to "get to the root of the problem"? What kind of plan did they have for restoring the Union?

The Big Question

Why did Thaddeus Stevens and the Radical Republicans decide to impeach Andrew Johnson?

Thaddeus Stevens

It's possible to understand what the Radical Republicans believed by getting to know one of their leaders, Thaddeus Stevens. Thaddeus grew up a poor boy in Vermont and moved to Gettysburg, Pennsylvania, at age twenty-four. He became a very successful and wealthy lawyer, but he never lost his sympathy for the poor and the **underdog**. Some say that his own physical handicap (he had a clubfoot that caused him to limp badly) gave him this sympathy.

> **Vocabulary**
>
> **underdog**, n. a person or group that is not likely to win

Thaddeus Stevens

Most of all, Stevens believed deeply in the words of Thomas Jefferson in the Declaration of Independence, "that all men are created equal," and that among their "unalienable rights" are "life, liberty, and the pursuit of happiness." Stevens lived his life by those words. He worked to get free public schools in Pennsylvania. He knew that education would help ordinary people in their "pursuit of happiness" just as it had helped him.

The special goal of Thad Stevens's life, though, was to secure those unalienable rights for African Americans. He was an abolitionist, and he acted on his beliefs. He used his skills as a lawyer on behalf of fugitive slaves. Although he was part of a group that wrote a new constitution for the state of Pennsylvania in 1838, he refused to sign it because it did not give the right to vote to the state's African American population.

So you see, Thad Stevens believed, as did the other Radical Republicans in Congress, that Reconstruction would be a failure unless it made Southern African Americans equal with whites. Were the former slaves uneducated? Then, give them schools. Did they have to depend completely on their old masters for work and do the master's bidding, as in the time of slavery? Then, give them land—forty acres and a mule. Did Southern whites deny them their rights—the right to vote, the right to be elected to office, the right to **testify** in court, and the right to do a hundred other things that white Southerners could do? Then, make the Southern states guarantee those rights in their new state constitutions, and don't let them back into the Union

> ### Vocabulary
> **testify,** v. to make a statement or provide evidence, usually in a court of law

174

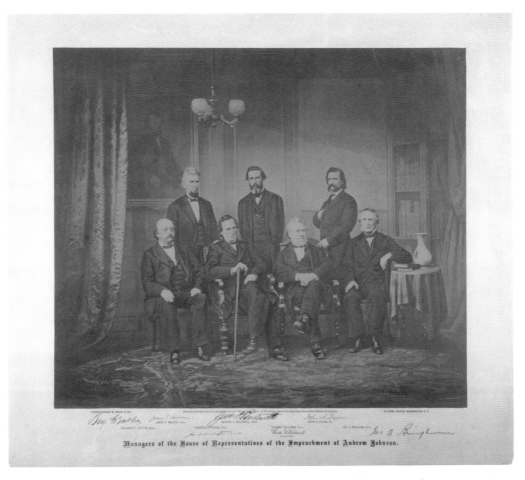

Managers of the House of Representatives of the Impeachment of Andrew Johnson.

Change would not come without a fight. This fight was led by the group of representatives seen here.

until they do. And at the same time, put those rights into the U.S. Constitution, where they would be beyond the reach of people who wanted to take them away.

Those were the ideas held by Thad Stevens and the Radical Republicans. And those were the ideas at the heart of Congressional Reconstruction. The Radical Republicans also desired to punish Southerners who had supported the rebellion against the United States.

In the spring of 1867 Congress, with the Radical Republicans in control, passed its plan for Reconstruction. Congressional Reconstruction, as it was called, began by turning the clock back to the end of the Civil War. The Radical Republicans threw out everything done under Presidential Reconstruction. This included the new state constitutions, the new state governments and all the laws they had passed (including the Black Codes), and all Southern representatives elected to Congress. Reconstruction would start all over again. "And," the Radicals said, "this time we will do it right."

Under Congressional Reconstruction, the U.S. Army was put in charge of the South until the Southern states were allowed to reenter the Union. Before the states could reenter, they had to do many things. They had to write new state constitutions, but this time African Americans as well as whites must take part in writing them. They had to elect new state governments, but this time African Americans had to be allowed to vote and to hold office. African Americans had to enjoy the same rights as white people.

People who had supported the rebellion against the United States were not allowed to take part in any of these activities. This included the hundreds of thousands who served in the Confederate armies. They had no say in writing their state constitutions. They could neither vote nor hold political office.

After a state adopted its new constitution and elected a new government, it must ratify the Fourteenth Amendment to the U.S. Constitution.

Once a state had done all these things, then and only then would it be received back into the Union. Then and only then would the U.S. troops leave that state.

"That," said the Radical Republicans, "is our plan for Reconstruction. That is what we insist the South must do. And woe be to anyone who tries to stand in our way."

The "anyone" the Radicals had in mind was President Andrew Johnson. They knew Johnson disagreed with their goals. They remembered that just the year before, he had advised the Southern states not to ratify the Fourteenth Amendment.

The Impeachment of President Johnson

The Radicals did not trust President Johnson. They believed he would ruin their plan for Reconstruction if he could. So, they passed several laws to limit the powers of the president.

President Johnson believed those laws were unconstitutional. He decided to ignore them. When he did that, the House of Representatives voted to **impeach** him. To *impeach* means to "put an officeholder on trial for wrongdoing." It's a way of getting rid of an officeholder before his term is over, if that officeholder has committed a serious offense. Under the U.S. Constitution, it is the job of the House of Representatives to impeach a president who is thought to be guilty of serious wrongdoing, or **"high crimes and misdemeanors."** If the House of Representatives votes to impeach, or bring charges against the president, then the president is put on trial before

> ### Vocabulary
>
> **impeach,** n.
> to accuse a government official of doing something wrong or improper
>
> **"high crimes and misdemeanors,"** (phrase) actions of misconduct by a government official, such as lying, abuse of power, or failing to perform job responsibilities

177

the U.S. Senate. If two-thirds of the senators find the president guilty of the charges brought against him, he or she is removed from office.

Some Radical Republicans, such as Thaddeus Stevens, wanted to impeach Johnson for a long time. But they couldn't impeach the president just because they didn't like his proposals. They needed a better reason than that. Now that Johnson had ignored the laws they had one.

The impeachment and trial of President Johnson lasted for two months in early 1868. While it lasted, it was the best show in town. The government printed tickets for admission, and people fell all over each other to get them. To no one's surprise, the House of Representatives voted to impeach the president. The case then moved to the Senate. There, it would take two-thirds of the Senate, or thirty-six senators, to vote "guilty as charged" in order to remove Johnson from office. The vote was close, extremely close. But the final count was thirty-five in favor of guilty, nineteen in favor of not guilty—one vote short of the number needed to remove the president from office. So, by that slim margin, Andrew Johnson was able to finish his term.

THE LAST SPEECH ON IMPEACHMENT—THADDEUS STEVENS CLOSING THE DEBATE IN THE HOUSE, MARCH 2.—[SKETCHED BY T. R. DAVIS.]

Thaddeus Stevens spoke out in favor of impeaching President Andrew Johnson.

Chapter 24
The South Under Reconstruction

New Governments Even though President Johnson escaped removal from office, he was powerless to stop Congressional Reconstruction. All over the defeated South, Southerners—this time African Americans as well as whites—began the job of writing new state constitutions, holding elections, and starting up their state governments again. The process took several years.

The Big Question

How did Reconstruction fail to give equality to African Americans?

Congressional Reconstruction led to big changes in the South. In each of the former Confederate states, African Americans were elected to serve in their state legislatures. In a few states, African Americans were elected to higher offices, such as **lieutenant governor**. Several African Americans were elected to serve in the U.S. House of Representatives and the U.S. Senate.

Vocabulary

lieutenant governor, n. an official in state government who ranks second to the governor

Joseph Hayne Rainey was the first African American to serve in the House of Representatives and the second to serve in Congress.

J. H. RAINEY,
EX-MEMBER OF CONGRESS.

Half of these African American officials were free persons before the war. Some of them were well-educated Northerners who moved to the South after the war ended. But about half of them had been slaves only a few years before. What an amazing turnaround that was!

Even though there were many African American officials and lawmakers, African Americans did not actually control these Southern states. Even under Congressional Reconstruction, most officeholders in the South continued to be white men.

Some of the white lawmakers and officials in the new Southern governments were actually Northerners who had gone south after the war. They went south for various reasons: to start farms or businesses, to help freedmen as teachers and ministers, or just to see whether they could make money from the South's troubles.

White Southerners disliked these Northern whites. They had an insulting name for them: carpetbaggers. A carpetbag is a cheap suitcase made of pieces of carpet. Southerners said these people came to the South with all their belongings in a carpetbag, which they hoped to fill with riches.

Most whites in the new governments, though, were people who had lived in the South all their lives. Some had never been in favor of secession. Some were business leaders. A good number were poor whites who were getting their first chance to gain power over the big planters who ruled the South. They thought the South would be better off if it changed some of its old ways.

Southerners who wanted to stick with the old ways had an insulting name for these people, too. They called them scalawags. That was the name Southerners gave to small, worthless farm animals.

The insults didn't matter. Serving together, the African American and white officials brought many improvements to their states. They rebuilt roads, railroads, and buildings that had been destroyed during the war. They helped the Southern economy to recover little by little. They also built hospitals and orphanages.

Probably most importantly, they started the first public school system in the South. There had been a few public schools in the South before the Civil War, but not many. In several of the Southern states, there were no public schools at all before the war. Now, in South Carolina alone, twelve thousand children went to public schools.

These African American and white officeholders, acting together, did one more thing, too. They ratified another amendment.

After the Civil War, schools were created for African Americans.

The Fifteenth Amendment says that no state can keep a person from voting because of his race or color. However, the Fifteenth Amendment did not give either African American or white women the right to vote right away. They did not get the right to vote until some years later.

Radical Republicans never reached their goal of full equality for African Americans. For many years, those who wanted to keep African Americans from voting found ways around the Fifteenth Amendment. But the Radical Republicans made an important start. The journey to reaching the goal of equal rights for all would be long and difficult, and even today it is not yet finished. Today, the United States is much closer to reaching that goal than ever before. And all Americans owe a debt of gratitude to the Radical Republicans for having started the country on that road.

The End of Reconstruction

Congressional Reconstruction lasted for only a few years because most white Southerners hated the new state governments. They felt these governments had been forced upon them against their will.

They were outraged that people who were once their slaves were now voting, holding office, and making laws. They opposed paying taxes for public schools that would educate African American children, even though those schools were educating their own children. They just couldn't accept the idea of a society in which white and African American people had equal rights.

African Americans in the South were threatened by groups like the Ku Klux Klan.

Southerners who felt this way were determined to win back control of their states and put an end to these changes. A number of them formed secret societies, such as the Ku Klux Klan. Wearing white sheets and hoods, members of the Ku Klux Klan rode through the countryside on horseback. They were violent and terrifying.

In the late 1860s and early 1870s, the federal government sent troops to stop the Ku Klux Klan and other secret groups like it. The government was successful, and the Klan almost disappeared. No one at that time knew that it would appear again more than forty years later. The next time it would preach its message of hatred against even more groups of Americans. The Klan still exists today.

Putting an end to the Klan, though, did not mean putting an end to white resistance to Congressional Reconstruction. Southerners formed other groups to keep African Americans from voting. These groups were not secret societies but societies that operated right out in the open. They warned that African Americans who voted would lose their jobs. They would not be able to buy goods on credit in the farm stores. They also threatened violence.

On election days, a few white thugs with rifles hung around the voting places. They sent a message to African American voters: Go ahead and vote, if you are ready to risk your life.

Those who wanted to get rid of the Reconstruction governments in the South finally succeeded in doing so. People in the North had their own concerns. They were growing weary of hearing about the trouble in the South and of being asked to do something about it. Strong leaders such as Thaddeus Stevens were gone. After a few years, the U.S. government gave back the vote to those who had served in the Confederate army. At the same time, white Southerners continued to use threats and violence to keep African Americans from voting.

In one Southern state after another, carpetbaggers, scalawags, and African Americans were voted out of office. They were replaced by white people who wanted to return to the old ways.

These issues came to a head in the election of 1876. Controversy over election results in some Southern states forced Congress to decide the election. Congress made a deal to give the presidency to the Republican candidate. As part of the deal, the U.S. government removed the last troops from the South. With that, Reconstruction was over.

Over the next several years, African Americans in the South lost nearly every right they had won during Reconstruction. With Reconstruction over, states passed **segregation** laws. These laws, put in place in the late 1870s onward, required the separation of whites and African Americans from each other. African Americans could no longer use the same restaurants, hotels, streetcars, theaters, and other public places that whites used. Or if they could, they had to sit in separate sections. These laws were known as Jim Crow laws. Segregation was informally practiced in much of the North, too, even though few Northern states had Jim Crow laws.

The end of Reconstruction also marked the end of fair trials of African Americans in the courts. And although the Fifteenth Amendment said that no state could deny a person's right to vote on account of their race or color, Southern states found ways to get around that. They passed laws that made it nearly impossible for African Americans to vote—and poor white people also. One such law required everyone who wanted to vote to pay a tax of two dollars. This kind of tax is called a poll tax. For many poor African Americans, and for poor whites, too, a two-dollar poll tax was nearly one week's wages!

One way to stop African American men from voting but allow poor whites to vote was the "grandfather clause." This stated that if a person's grandfather was a slave and could not vote, neither could they.

Another law said that in order to vote, people had to pass a test to prove they could read and understand the state's constitution. It was up to a local official to decide who passed the test and who didn't. Generally, that local official was a white man who was determined to keep African Americans from voting. So no matter how well an African American could read, he often was not allowed to pass the test. When a white person couldn't read, he was usually allowed to vote anyway.

And for any African American still thinking about casting a vote, there remained the threat of violence or of losing one's job. Before long, there were few African American voters in the South and no African American officeholders.

African Americans would have to wait many more years before they would really enjoy the equal rights that the Declaration of Independence and the Fourteenth and Fifteenth Amendments promised them.

It's important to understand just how significant the Civil War was in terms of keeping the United States together as a whole. This was the main goal from beginning to end for those who fought for the Union. They believed strongly in holding on to the promise of the founding generation, keeping alive the example of democracy, and enabling the United States to become a world power. For these reasons, they were willing to take up arms against their fellow countrymen.

In the 1960s, African Americans and white Americans fought back against laws that had denied freedom to so many for so long.

Glossary

A

abolitionist, n. a person who worked to end slavery during the 1700s and 1800s **(27)**

acre, n. an area of land that measures 4,840 square yards **(161)**

admission, n. permission to join a group or enter a place **(44)**

ammunition, n. bullets or shells **(72)**

arsenal, n. a place where weapons and other military equipment are stored **(64)**

B

battlefront, n. the place where soldiers fight during a battle **(128)**

bind, v. to tie up **(150)**

"Black Codes," (phrase) laws passed in Southern states to limit the freedoms of African Americans after the Civil War **(170)**

blockade, n. a military strategy aimed at preventing people and goods from entering or leaving an area **(84)**

bombardment, n. a continuous attack with bombs, missiles, or other types of ammunition **(73)**

bonus, n. extra money that is added to a person's pay **(117)**

C

cabinet, n. a group of government officials who advise the president **(144)**

caution, n. carefulness; efforts made to avoid danger or risk **(92)**

character, n. the qualities that make up the personality and behavior of a person or a country **(22)**

civil rights, n. the rights that all citizens are supposed to have according to the Constitution and its amendments **(6)**

colonel, n. a high-ranking military official **(106)**

compromise, n. when each side in a dispute gives up some of their demands to reach an agreement **(18)**

Confederate, adj. of or relating to the eleven states that seceded from the Union to form a new and separate republic **(68)**

consecrate, v. to declare something sacred or holy **(137)**

consent, n. approval or agreement **(12)**

constitutional, adj. allowed or legal under the terms of the U.S. Constitution **(54)**

"constitutional amendment," (phrase) an official change or addition to the Constitution **(27)**

cultivate, v. to help grow **(9)**

D

decisiveness, n. an ability to make decisions quickly **(94)**

decree, n. a formal order or statement, usually by a government **(105)**

defensive, adj. designed to keep safe or protect against attack **(79)**

deliverance, n. the action of rescuing someone or setting them free **(16)**

dissolve, v. to end something, such as an organization **(63)**

draft, n. a system that requires individuals to serve in the military **(117)**

E

emancipation, n. the act of setting someone or something free **(102)**

endure, v. to last **(63)**

exercise, v. to actively use or do something **(62)**

F

fugitive, n. a person who runs away or hides to avoid capture **(46)**

G

governor, n. the elected leader of a state in the United States **(140)**

H

hallow, v. to honor or respect (137)

"high crimes and misdemeanors," (phrase) actions of misconduct by a government official, such as lying, abuse of power, or failing to perform job responsibilities (177)

I

impeach, n. to accuse a government official of doing something wrong or improper (177)

L

legislature, n. the part of the government responsible for making laws (21)

lieutenant governor, n. an official in state government who ranks second to the governor (180)

M

malice, n. a desire to hurt another person (150)

manpower, n. the number of people available for a task (86)

"manufactured good," (phrase) an item made in large numbers for sale or trade (142)

manufacturing, n. the production of items in large numbers for sale or trade (36)

mill, n. a building or group of buildings where goods are produced (36)

mystify, v. to confuse (108)

N

natural rights, n. rights that all people are born with and that cannot be taken away by the government (64)

O

outwit, v. to outsmart; to win by using trickery (17)

P

peninsula, adj. of or related to a piece of land that sticks out into a body of water (94)

preserve, v. to keep or save (70)

R

racist, n. a person who believes one race of people is superior to, or better than, another (154)

radical, adj. favoring large or widespread changes (170)

ratify, v. to approve (166)

reconcile, v. to return to a friendly relationship after a conflict (164)

Reconstruction, n. in the United States, the period of rebuilding after the Civil War (168)

resist, v. to fight against; oppose (14)

resistance, n. the act of taking a stand against something by way of words or actions (14)

righteous, adj. moral or virtuous (105)

rural, adj. relating to the countryside (39)

S

secede, v. to formally withdraw membership (45)

secret agent, n. a spy; a person who collects and reports secret information about other governments or countries (154)

"secretary of war," (phrase) the government official responsible for planning and executing wars (93)

segregation, n. the act of keeping people separate, usually on the basis of race (187)

self-evident, adj. obvious (5)

senator, n. a member of the Senate in the Congress of the United States (44)

siege, n. a battle strategy in which enemy soldiers surround a building or place so that those under attack cannot receive supplies; a blockade (132)

slavery, n. a system in which people are legally owned by another and forced to work without pay (4)

spy, n. a person who collects secret information about an enemy, often while in enemy territory (126)

statehood, n. the condition of being a state in the United States (20)

states' rights, n. political powers that belong to state governments under the Constitution; also, the belief that the federal government should have less power and state governments should have more power **(138)**

strategy, n. a plan of action created to achieve a specific goal **(84)**

stronghold, n. a place that is strengthened or fortified against an attack **(132)**

substitute, n. a person or thing that acts in place of another **(118)**

Supreme Court, n. the highest court in the land **(60)**

surgeon, n. a doctor who is trained to perform surgery, or operations **(128)**

surveyor, n. a worker who measures and examines land **(31)**

T

tactic, n. an action used to reach a goal **(109)**

telegraph, v. to communicate over long distances by sending signals through wires **(134)**

territory, n. an area of land **(18)**

testify, v. to make a statement or provide evidence, usually in a court of law **(174)**

"tide of battle," (idiom) the way that a conflict is going **(76)**

U

unalienable, adj. unable to be taken away or denied **(5)**

underdog, n. a person or group that is not likely to win **(172)**

Underground Railroad, n. a secret organization that helped slaves escape to freedom **(29)**

Union, n. the states that made up the United States of America; during the Civil War the states that supported the U.S. government **(20)**

upper hand, n. control or advantage **(77)**

urban, adj. relating to a city **(39)**

V

veto, v. to reject or refuse to approve a law **(170)**

volunteer, n. a person who chooses or offers to serve in the military; a person who offers to complete a task or participate in an event without pay **(92)**

W

warehouse, n. a large building where goods are stored **(128)**